Paideia Problems
and Possibilities

PAIDEIA PROBLEMS AND POSSIBILITIES

MORTIMER J. ADLER

ON BEHALF OF THE MEMBERS OF THE PAIDEIA GROUP

MACMILLAN PUBLISHING COMPANY
NEW YORK

COLLIER MACMILLAN PUBLISHERS
LONDON

Macmillan Publishing Company
866 Third Avenue, New York, N.Y. 10022
Collier Macmillan Canada, Inc.

Library of Congress Cataloging in Publication Data

Adler, Mortimer Jerome, 1902–
Paideia problems and possibilities.

1. Education, Humanistic—United States—Philosophy.
2. Education, Elementary—United States—Aims and objectives.   3. Education, Secondary—United States—Aims and objectives.   I. Title.
LC1011.A34 1983   370'.973   83-12025
ISBN 0-02-500220-1
ISBN 0-02-013050-3 (pbk.)

First Macmillan Paperbacks Edition 1983

10 9 8 7 6 5 4 3 2 1

Printed in the United States of America

Paideia Problems and Possibilities is also published in a hardcover edition by Macmillan Publishing Company.

The Paideia Group wishes to express its gratitude to the Atlantic Richfield Foundation, Richard King Mellon Foundation, The Hunt Foundation, The Lauder Foundation, and the Samuel I. Newhouse Foundation Inc. for financial support needed to carry out this work.

TO

THE YOUTH OF AMERICA

P A I D E I A (py-dee-a) from the Greek *pais, paidos:*
the upbringing of a child. (Related to pedagogy and
pediatrics.) In an extended sense, the equivalent of
the Latin *humanitas* (from which "the humanities"),
signifying the general learning that should be the
possession of all human beings.

Members of the Paideia Group

MORTIMER J. ADLER, *Chairman*
> Director, Institute for Philosophical Research; Chairman, Board of Editors, Encyclopaedia Britannica

JACQUES BARZUN, former Provost, Columbia University; Literary Adviser, Charles Scribner's Sons, New York

OTTO BIRD, former head, General Program of Liberal Studies, University of Notre Dame, Indiana

LEON BOTSTEIN, President, Bard College, Annandale-on-Hudson, New York; President, Simon's Rock of Bard College, Great Barrington, Massachusetts

ERNEST L. BOYER, President, The Carnegie Foundation for the Advancement of Teaching, Washington, D.C.

NICHOLAS L. CAPUTI, Principal, Skyline High School, Oakland, California

DOUGLASS CATER, Senior Fellow, Aspen Institute for Humanistic Studies; President, Washington College, Chestertown, Maryland

DONALD COWAN, former President, University of Dallas; Fellow, Dallas Institute of Humanities and Cultures, Texas

ALONZO A. CRIM, Superintendent, Atlanta Public Schools, Georgia

CLIFTON FADIMAN, Author and critic

DENNIS GRAY, Deputy Director, Council for Basic Education, Washington, D.C.

RICHARD HUNT, Senior Lecturer and Director of the Andrew W. Mellon Faculty Fellowships Program, Harvard University, Cambridge, Massachusetts

Members of the Paideia Group

RICHARD LA POINTE, former Superintendent of Schools, Contra Costa County, California; Kellogg National Fellow; Senior Visiting Scholar, Cambridge University, England

RUTH B. LOVE, General Superintendent of Schools, Chicago Board of Education

JAMES NELSON, Director, Wye Institute, Inc., Queenstown, Maryland

JAMES O'TOOLE, Professor of Management, Graduate School of Business Administration, University of Southern California, Los Angeles

THEODORE T. PUCK, President and Director, Eleanor Roosevelt Institute for Cancer Research, Inc.; Professor of Biochemistry, Biophysics, and Genetics, University of Colorado, Denver

ADOLPH W. SCHMIDT, former Chairman, Board of Visitors and Governors of St. John's College, Annapolis, Maryland and Santa Fe, New Mexico

ADELE SIMMONS, President, Hampshire College, Amherst, Massachusetts

THEODORE R. SIZER, Chairman, A Study of High Schools; former Headmaster, Phillips Academy-Andover, Massachusetts

CHARLES VAN DOREN, Associate Director, Institute for Philosophical Research

GERALDINE VAN DOREN, Senior Fellow, Institute for Philosophical Research; Secretary, Paideia Project

JOHN VAN DOREN, Senior Fellow, Institute for Philosophical Research; Executive Editor, *Great Ideas Today*

Contents

Preface

THIS SEQUEL to *The Paideia Proposal* is called for by the nationwide response that the proposal elicited.

The Paideia Proposal persuaded a great many of its readers and listeners as well as those who engaged in discussion with members of the Paideia Group, the proposed reform of basic schooling in the United States aimed in the right direction and that the steps recommended for moving toward the goal would be effective in achieving it.

But those thus persuaded naturally raised questions and posed problems that the little book entitled *The Paideia Proposal* perforce left unanswered. The twenty-two persons of the Paideia Group thought that the first order of business was to address educators, administrators, teachers, school boards, parents, and others concerned with the state of the schools and enlist their support for a radical reform of the public school system, and the private schools as well.

The Paideia Group was also of the opinion that until evidence was forthcoming that the concerned public was persuaded by this appeal, there was little point in dealing with specific questions arising from the reform proposed or with the details of its possible implementation.

The evidence looked for has now been amply provided. We are therefore encouraged to proceed to the next order of business, which is to try to answer questions and discuss problems of implementation. That is the purpose of the present book.

In *The Paideia Proposal* we promised to supply a follow-up book of essays by members of the group, which might serve as guidelines for developing the various elements in the curricular framework there outlined. That follow-up book, to be entitled *The Paideia Program,* is in preparation and will be published shortly after this one.

Paideia Problems and Possibilities

1
Questions, Not Objections

SIDE BY SIDE with the evidence of wide interest and approval, the Paideia Group has of course heard from a number of teachers, principals, educational administrators, and professors of education, not to mention parents, public officials, and other concerned persons, who take issue with the proposal.

Some think that its principles—the ends or goals it sets up and the measures it recommends for achieving them—are unattainable, illusory. Others who regard the objectives as attainable, nonetheless reject them as fundamentally misguided. Others assent to the goals aimed at, but challenge the means recommended as not well devised or adequate for the purpose.

This book does not undertake to reply to such objections and challenges. To reply would mean to survey contemporary society and the history of its cultural institutions for the past hundred years. It would promote debate when it is action that is urgently called for. The present statement therefore confines itself to the questions raised by those whose response to the Paideia proposal is favorable—those who approve of the ends to be served and generally concur in the choice of means for establishing a truly democratic system of basic schooling in this country.

Addressed to them, this book tries, in Chapter 4, to provide the clarification they seek by the questions they ask about the

1

Paideia principles. In Chapter 5, it deals with the difficult problems of implementing those principles in practice.

Everyone understands the distinction between architects who plan buildings and construction engineers who erect them; and between the work of such policy makers as school boards or boards of education and school administrators who are charged with the execution of plans and policies. A similar distinction exists between those of us who have been engaged in the formulation of the Paideia proposal and those on the front line of educational change who have expressed a desire to implement the Paideia program.

We are aware that it is much easier to state general principles and to formulate general policies than it is to carry them into execution. We also recognize the different but quite complementary contributions made by those who perform these different functions in their joint efforts to achieve a desired practical result.

Thinking in general terms about the reform of basic schooling is akin to architectural planning or like policy making in other spheres of activity. By itself such thinking is insufficient. Even the clearest definition of the objectives of basic schooling and the most comprehensive statement of the general means to be employed for the sake of those objectives leaves one more step to be taken—the step that precedes action, at which point decisions must be made about the particular means or measures to be chosen under the particular circumstances that surround action at a given time and place.

The members of the Paideia group have served so far as educational planners, theorists, or, if you will, as educational philosophers engaged in thinking about the ultimate ends and the means thereto, but they have stated the ends and means only in the most general terms.

School boards, boards of education, together with the superintendents, principals, and teachers under their jurisdiction, must now take up where we leave off. If persuaded by us, they must now try to put the Paideia principles into practice. We, in turn, must now try to help them by answering their questions and suggesting solutions to their problems.

2
Paideia Principles Revisited:
The Objectives or Goals

THE PAIDEIA GROUP has been primarily, though not exclusively, concerned with the twelve years of basic schooling that are compulsory for all children in this country. Some children may take only eleven years to complete the course; others may take thirteen; but not all go on to further, optional schooling in advanced educational institutions. Basic schooling is the only institutional education that is compulsory; it is the only schooling that is common to all.

This being so, our concern is, once again, primarily with what basic schooling should do for all, without regard to whether they do or do not go on to colleges and universities, or technical and professional schools. While basic schooling should prepare for such further schooling for those who seek it, that ought not to be its primary aim. In fact, it has no need to be, for if basic schooling does the job that it should do for all, it will at the same time fully serve the needs of those who elect to go further.

The point just made follows from the fundamental proposition that the objectives of basic schooling should be the same for all because what is common to all is more fundamental than the ways in which human being differ from one another as individuals. These common traits are: their common humanity, their personal dignity, their human rights and aspirations, and

5

the futures to which they are all destined as equal members of our society.

They are all destined to enjoy the equal status of citizenship with suffrage. They should all be able to look forward to earning a living by doing the best work of which they are capable. They are all promised a longer and healthier life than their forbears. In our technologically advanced economy they will all have many more hours and years of free time for the pursuits of leisure whereby they can grow mentally, morally, and spiritually. Each, if given the basic schooling that all deserve, should be able to make as much of himself or herself as possible and enjoy a quality of life that by common consent belongs to every human being.

A constitutional democracy such as ours does not rest only on the principle of political equality—the equal status of citizenship. It is also committed to the principle of equal educational opportunity—equal in quality, not just in quantity. The one without the other makes democracy a sham and a delusion.

Moreover, a technologically advanced society is subject to radical changes in the production of goods and services. These changes in turn require a work force that is prepared for flexible and intelligent adjustment to novel demands for skill and comprehension.

A hundred years ago human beings died in a world that, with respect to jobs and employment, closely resembled the world into which they had been born. That is no longer the case, and it will be even less so in the years immediately ahead. Trained competence for a single type of work could be justified at the beginning of this century when the needs of society differed little from those served by apprenticeships in the era of guilds. That kind of training is no longer justified. It is no longer useful. On the contrary, practicality now calls for the opposite kind of preparation—preparation for varied and changing tasks, a preparation that should be given in basic schooling and that all should receive. Highly specialized technical training, wherever useful, comes later.

Labor-saving devices have progressively reduced the hours of work required for the functioning of the economy and have proportionately increased the amount of free time at the disposal of everyone who earns a living. A hundred years ago, or even in the first decades of this century, a vast majority of those employed worked six or seven days a week, ten to twelve hours a day; they began to work at a much earlier age and usually died before enjoying surcease from toil. It would have been folly then to regard their basic schooling as preparation for any form of self-development.

Lacking time in their lives for anything beyond toil and the things that kept them alive, they were denied the opportunity to make decent, human, civilized lives for themselves. They were drudges, stultified by their drudgery.

All that has been changed. Now and to an ever increasing degree in the future, even supposing full employment, ample free time, with all the opportunities that it affords, will be the rule rather than the exception.

We are now facing serious unemployment because of a worldwide economic recession. We may well face even more serious unemployment in the future because of technological advances in production. But that problem is for society and the economy to solve, not the schools.

What basic schooling can contribute to the solution is to give the young the most general, the least particularized, preparation for performing productive work. This means learning early the art of adapting to changing forms and conditions of work. Schooling can do this only by developing those basic skills that *everyone* needs to do almost *any* kind of work.

It is for these intensely practical reasons that the threefold ends or objectives of basic schooling, as Paideia conceives them, should be the same for all. In an ascending order of importance, they are: (1) preparation for earning a living; (2) preparation for the duties of citizenship in a democracy, in which the citizens are the ruling class and holders of public office; and (3) preparation for self-development, which cannot occur without continued learning and personal growth during maturity after all schooling, basic or advanced, has been completed.

Only the third of these objectives needs further comment. It is needed because of the widely prevalent supposition that the education of a human being occurs in school and is completed there. Nothing could be further from the truth. Even if schooling at all levels were of the highest degree of excellence imaginable, it would still be true that no one can become an educated human being during the years spent at school. That is simply because those are the years of everyone's immaturity. The immaturity that inevitably accompanies being young presents an insuperable obstacle to becoming educated.

To regard a high school diploma, or a college or graduate degree, as certifying the completion of one's education is to make a mockery of the whole process. To call a young person who holds such certificates an educated human being is as self-contradictory as to refer to a round square. Schooling is a phase in the educative process. Basic schooling is the first and most important phase. It must be conceived, first and foremost, as preparation for continued learning throughout the years of one's life. Education begins after that schooling, or additional schooling, has been completed. It is essentially self-education. And self-education will be well or poorly done in proportion to the quality of schooling that prepares for it.

To discharge this obligation, basic schooling must do three things. It must (1) give the young an introduction to the world of learning; (2) give them all the skills of learning; and (3) give them the incentives and the stimulation to continue learning without end after schooling is ended. Or, to put it in other words, basic schooling must acquaint a person with what can be learned, train the natural aptitudes for learning, and reinforce the desire to learn that is inherent in everyone at birth. Deficient basic schooling kills that desire and prevents self-education forever after. But if given the what, the how, and the why of learning, all but the pathologically retarded are set on the path to becoming generally educated persons—a goal to which everyone who has a proper respect for his or her human gifts should aspire.

The three objectives of basic schooling, when offered to all the children, will promote the general welfare of this country in a number of ways that should be briefly mentioned before we turn to the means and measures required.

First, basic schooling thus directed will be an indispensable factor, though not the only factor, in bringing to full fruition the promises and benefits conferred upon a people by the institutions of political democracy. Its guarantees of liberty, equality, and justice for all, through the securing of their human rights, depend ultimately on the spread of intelligence, knowledge, judgment, and understanding. These qualities, which are potential in all human beings, are developed by proper schooling—schooling that informs and trains the mind.

We have said that *The Paideia Proposal* is an educational manifesto. Like the book from which it derives inspiration, John Dewey's *Democracy and Education,* it takes democracy seriously. It should be said, in addition, that the reason why the two words conjoined in the title of Dewey's epoch-making book could not have been put together much earlier than the year in which it appeared—1916—lies in the fact that *political democracy,* conceived as *constitutional government with truly universal suffrage and with the securing of all human rights,* did not exist on paper, much less in practice, at the beginning of this century.

What most Americans do not recognize or fully appreciate is that political democracy, in these terms, is an innovation in human history that is less than fifty years old. It came into existence through a series of constitutional amendments and juridical measures that began in the second decade of this century and continued through successive decades until the very recent past. With these legal advances in the direction of political equality and with the expansion of human rights to include economic as well as political rights, social, economic, and political democracy gradually emerged on paper, but it has still not been fully implemented. Much remains for the future to accomplish.

No wonder, then, that a truly democratic program of education in the public and private schools of this country should have lagged behind and still awaits establishment. Until the commitment to democracy becomes both widely prevalent and genuinely serious and is accompanied by an understanding of its novelty, which is to say its challenge to deeply ingrained prejudices, the appeal to make basic schooling democratic could not succeed.

Our hope is that the time is at last ripe for such success. The nationwide response to the appeal of *The Paideia Proposal* has strengthened that hope.

Second, the proposed reform of basic schooling will contribute to the prosperity of a technologically advanced and rapidly changing economy. American industry and business are now hampered by having to use a work force which is not prepared for the tasks that men and women must perform once computers and robots have taken over what were formerly human occupations.

Third, our national security requires armed forces similarly prepared. Technological advances in weaponry call for troops— on land, sea, and in the air—possessed of a degree of schooling not needed for military service in the first and second world wars. And the new troops must be competent to learn and re-learn indefinitely as weapons and equipment change.

Fourth, if we are concerned about not only preserving our cultural tradition but also about enhancing and adding to it, nothing less than the kind and quality of basic schooling we recommend will serve the purpose. Should we fail in this regard, the number of generally educated human beings in the coming generations will shrink almost to the vanishing point. General culture is no elitist property; it is a common heritage that everyone shares in, often unconsciously and at every level of enjoyment. What chance is there that general culture will survive with a dwindling number of generally cultivated persons?

Finally, each individual's right to a genuine opportunity for the pursuit of happiness requires schooling of a high quality.

11

If we conceive this pursuit as an effort to make a good life for oneself—a life that is enriched by the possession of all the things that are really good for a human being to enjoy—it should be clear that the desire for such things and the power to attain them will remain dormant and undeveloped without the early guidance of good schooling.

3
Paideia Principles Revisited: The General Means

FOR THE DESIRED OBJECTIVES to be achieved, and with an eye to the ultimate social and human goals that they serve, what are the means to be employed? What in general is the character of these means?

The first thing to be said about the means in general is that there should be a required course of study for all. To this principle there is only one exception: the elective choice of a foreign language. That one choice should itself be mandatory: the study of at least one foreign language should be required for all.

This means that the course of study should be a single track along which all move—at different speeds, perhaps, and under different conditions. There may be regional modifications of the required course of study. But these differences, necessary for the accommodation of the sameness in the course of study to differences among students or regions, must not result in a differentiation of tracks along which different groups of students move. The only result should be a differentiation of the ways that differing students move along the same track.

Only brief mention need be made here of two devices proposed for dealing with individual differences in native endowment and in environmental or cultural backgrounds. One is the recommendation of varying amounts of pre-school tutoring for children according to their needs and the other is the recommendation of supplementary instruction and additional coaching for those who fall behind in any phase of the program.

What must be more fully explained, because it was not discussed in *The Paideia Proposal,* is our recommendation about the grouping of students for instruction. Such grouping should be based on success in mastering and completing skills and tasks; it should not be based solely on chronological age. The evidence is overwhelming that individuals grow intellectually at differing rates and at different times. Grouping students by age tends to discourage some and inordinately swells the heads of others. The true objective is a measure of mastery by all, not advancement from grade to grade by age and at the same speed for all.

In the nature of things, the recommendation of achievement grouping, as opposed to age grouping, will apply to certain elements in the course of study, not to all. It applies particularly to learning mathematics and the natural sciences and possibly less to learning about history, geography, and social institutions.

In other areas of the curriculum, especially in physical training, in manual training, and in seminars devoted to the understanding of books and other works of art, age grouping, far from being an impediment, may be highly desirable, for social as well as for educational reasons.

The prescription of one required course of study for all children in the twelve years of compulsory basic schooling *does not lay down a single, detailed curriculum to be adopted nationwide.* To do so would be unpardonably presumptuous in a country, such as ours, which is radically pluralistic in culture and in its educational system. The determination in detail of one required course of study for all must be left to each of the fifteen thousand or more autonomous school boards or boards of education that wield authority over schooling within their jurisdiction.

The Paideia Proposal's prescription of the means (the means in general, not in detail) for achieving the goals aimed at by basic schooling goes no further than to *chart the framework within which any adequate course of study should be constructed*. The nationwide sameness for all students resides solely in the sameness of this recommended framework, not in any sameness of detail as to the materials to be used, the precise organization of the curriculum, and other particular measures and methods to be devised. These will be inevitably and also desirably different in different school districts.

Before sketching the common framework, it is necessary to point out that prescribing a curricular framework is unavoidable because it provides the only means by which the ends in view can be achieved. The country has tried diversity of aims and means and that has failed. A common aim and common general means are now imperative. The three objectives delineated on page 9 as the goals of basic schooling cannot be achieved by courses of study that do not include all the elements set forth in the Paideia framework.

The prescription is relatively simple. Difficulties arise only in its execution.

It calls for the inclusion of three kinds of learning and three kinds of teaching throughout the twelve years of basic schooling. When we insist that the course of study *must* include all

15

three modes of learning and teaching in order to be effective, that prescription seems to us as indisputable as the recommendation of a balanced diet for bodily health and vigor.

No one with a rudimentary knowledge of biology would quarrel with the statement that a sound diet *must* include fats, carbohydrates, and proteins in certain proportions. This dietary prescription, like our curricular prescription, is only the framework for a sound diet. It leaves undetermined the choice of particular foods and the arrangement of meals.

Wrong food choices and haphazard meal times and menus can be criticized by pointing out either that one or another of the essential ingredients of a sound diet has been left out or that they are not properly proportioned.

Similarly, anyone with a rudimentary knowledge of psychology—knowing the ways in which the mind can be improved and the factors involved in its improvement—will recognize at once the soundness of the comparable educational prescription. Having only one kind, or even two kinds, of learning and teaching in the course of study is as detrimental to mental growth as having only fats, or only fats and carbohydrates, in one's daily diet is harmful to the body.

Here precisely is our criticism of the curriculum, even in our better schools and for our better students: *they are deprived of modes of learning and teaching needed for their mental growth and vigor.*

Stated with maximum brevity, the three modes of learning are as follows: (1) the acquisition of organized *knowledge* in three fields of subject matter—language, literature, and the fine arts; mathematics and natural science; history, geography, and the study of social institutions; (2) the development of intellectual *skills*, all of which are skills of learning and of thinking; and (3) the enhancement of the *understanding* of basic ideas and values. In short: knowledge, skills, understanding.

It will be noticed that only the first of these three modes of learning involves branches of knowledge designated by the names of subject-matter. The first of these three modes of learning results in knowing *that* or knowing *what*. The second results in knowing *how* (for every skill, art, or technique consists in knowing how to do something well). The third mode of learning, which aims at enhanced understanding, consists in knowing *why* and *wherefore*.

The three modes of teaching correlated with these three modes of learning are (1) the didactic, which is teaching by telling or lecturing, aided by textbooks, manuals, recitations, demonstrations, quizzes, and examinations; (2) coaching, which is teaching by supervising performances to attain skills (for every skill is acquired by habit formation, and good habits, which skills are, result from repeated acts under the guidance of a seasoned performer who is a coach); (3) Socratic or "maieutic" teaching, which is teaching by asking or questioning (not telling or lecturing, and certainly not coaching). Socratic teaching is most effectively done in seminars, in which students engage in free discussion that is kept on track by a leader, the materials discussed being either books (books that are not textbooks) or productions of quality in other fields of art and thought.

Readers of *The Paideia Proposal* will remember the diagram on page 23 of Chapter 4 (that diagram is reproduced on the next page). It depicts the framework within which any sound course of study for twelve years of basic schooling should

	COLUMN ONE	COLUMN TWO	COLUMN THREE
Goals	ACQUISITION OF ORGANIZED KNOWLEDGE	DEVELOPMENT OF INTELLECTUAL SKILLS – SKILLS OF LEARNING	ENLARGED UNDERSTANDING OF IDEAS AND VALUES
	by means of	by means of	by means of
Means	DIDACTIC INSTRUCTION LECTURES AND RESPONSES TEXTBOOKS AND OTHER AIDS in three areas of subject-matter	COACHING, EXERCISES, AND SUPERVISED PRACTICE in the operations of	MAIEUTIC OR SOCRATIC QUESTIONING AND ACTIVE PARTICIPATION in the
Areas Operations and Activities	LANGUAGE, LITERATURE, AND THE FINE ARTS MATHEMATICS AND NATURAL SCIENCE HISTORY, GEOGRAPHY, AND SOCIAL STUDIES	READING, WRITING, SPEAKING, LISTENING CALCULATING, PROBLEM-SOLVING OBSERVING, MEASURING, ESTIMATING EXERCISING CRITICAL JUDGMENT	DISCUSSION OF BOOKS (NOT TEXTBOOKS) AND OTHER WORKS OF ART AND INVOLVEMENT IN ARTISTIC ACTIVITIES e.g., MUSIC, DRAMA, VISUAL ARTS

THE THREE COLUMNS DO NOT CORRESPOND TO SEPARATE COURSES, NOR IS ONE KIND OF TEACHING AND LEARNING NECESSARILY CONFINED TO ANY ONE CLASS

18

be constructed. In the concluding pages of that chapter, it was said that the program recommended was offered as a model. It can be adapted in a variety of ways to the diverse circumstances of different schools or school systems. Our recommendation is not a monolithic program to be adopted uniformly everywhere.

In other words, the diagram charts the general means for achieving the desired objectives. It leaves open the detailed determination that must be made in applying the means in general to a particular, local situation.

It was said a few pages back that while the prescription itself is relatively simple, difficulties arise in carrying it out. They do not arise from any native incapacity on the part of students. All children can learn and can make progress in all three modes of learning. That most students do not do so now results not from incapacity on their part, but rather from the deprivations they suffer at the outset of their schooling, from inadequate courses of study, and from inadequate teaching.

Most teachers are currently trained to do only the didactic kind of teaching. A relatively small number have been given some competence in coaching the intellectual skills—largely in the language arts. Few, if any, have received training in the art of teaching Socratically, and the few who have the requisite skill exercise it not by curricular plan, but spontaneously, from natural gifts and propensities. They are the rare birds of the teaching profession as currently constituted.

The misdirection of teacher training and deficiencies in preparation for teaching are not the only difficulties to overcome in order to put the Paideia program into practice. Another difficulty lies in the kind of daily schedule that obtains in most schools at present—the fifty-minute class period that is appropriate only for the first mode of learning and teaching. If retained without modification, it would defeat attempts to introduce the second and third modes of learning and teaching, which require other allotments of time. They also require other types of classroom arrangements. The usual classroom with students sitting in rows and the teacher standing behind or in front of his or her desk simply will not work for teachers engaged in coaching students or for students and teachers engaged in seminar discussions.

The diagram on page 18 does not exhaust the requirements of a sound curriculum for basic schooling. The prescription of the general means also calls for three auxiliary elements: (1) twelve years of physical education; (2) six or eight years of manual training in the household arts of cooking and sewing, carpentry, machine repair, typing, etc.; and (3) one or two years of a general introduction to the world of work—a panoramic survey of the vocational future, involving an acquaintance with the diversity of careers, their requirements, opportunities, and rewards.

Training in the manual arts is not for the sake of earning a living by becoming proficient in one or another of them. It is as much mind-training—a development of intellectual skills—as is training in the language arts, in mathematical operations, in scientific method, and in the use of computers.

So, too, the requirement that a second language be studied for four to six years (with the choice of language being left open) is not for the sake of some use to which a second language can be put, but rather for the sake of skill in the language arts themselves—the skills of reading and writing, speaking and listening.

With regard to the principal elements in the prescription—the three modes of learning and of teaching—one important point must be repeated. Though knowledge of subject-matters, the possession of intellectual skills, and the understanding of what is known and how skills should be used, are distinct one from another, they cannot be separated in their development or use. The three modes of learning and teaching must be related—more than that, integrated—at every stage of the educational process.

Since the students are asked to engage in all three modes of learning in an integrated fashion, the teachers must show an ability to perform all three modes of teaching. The only specialization expected of them is in this or that subject-matter, with respect to which they need special competence as didactic teachers. But it is clear that they, no less than their students, must possess the intellectual skills as well as have the ability to coach students in developing them. Again, no less than the students, they must be seekers of understanding in the discussion of basic ideas and values. This implies being able to formulate the kind of questions and challenges that are needed to make a seminar lively and productive of results.

The point being made is understood when one says "no less than the students." In the second and third modes of learning, the obligation of the teacher consists in having the common intellectual skills to a higher degree and in having a fuller, because more mature, understanding of basic ideas and values.

To sum up, let us repeat here what was said in the closing pages of Chapter 4 of *The Paideia Proposal:*

> The program recommended in the preceding pages is offered
> as a model. It can be adapted in a variety of ways to the diverse

21

circumstances of different schools or school systems. *Our recommendation is not a monolithic program to be adopted uniformly everywhere.*

But the model does insist, for its validity, on the presence in all schools or school systems of the Three Columns—on the establishing of the three modes of learning and the three modes of teaching. The precise way in which that is to be accomplished will be determined by school boards and administrators in the light of the populations with which they are dealing and with reference to a variety of other relevant circumstances.

The system of public education in this country has always been pluralistic and should remain so. Preserving pluralism need not and should not prevent the adoption by *all* our schools of the central features of our model as an ideal to be realized in a variety of specifically different ways.

This cannot be conscientiously accomplished simply by introducing in some form the Three Columns of Learning. It also calls for the elimination of many things that now clutter up the school day. At the very least, their elimination is necessary to make room for what should displace them.

The foregoing summary of the general means for achieving the ends of basic schooling has so far been confined to the prescription of a common framework within which a course of study should be constructed. There remain a few other general considerations that lead us to further general prescriptions that are equally inescapable.

(1) In every school, the principal should function as the principal teacher—the headmaster—not just as the chief administrator performing clerical and other tasks completely external to teaching and learning. A school is a community and, like any other community, it needs leadership. Since its reason

for existence is teaching and learning, educational leadership must be provided by its principal. If the burden of administrative duties and clerical tasks threatens to take too much of his or her time and energy, that burden must be shouldered by assistants who need not be educators, but who are responsible to the *principal educator* in carrying out their assigned tasks.

(2) Teachers must understand their role in the learning process. They misconceive it when they think of themselves as the primary cause of learning on the part of students. They are at best only instrumental causes of learning. The primary cause is always and only the activity of the student's mind. When that cause is not operative, genuine learning does not take place. When teachers regard themselves as imparting the knowledge they have in their own minds by somehow getting it into the minds of students, the result is a stuffing of the memory, not a growth of the mind. This is not to say that rote-learning or memorization should be completely eliminated. A modicum of it is useful, even indispensable.

Memory-stuffing is not likely to occur in the mode of teaching that is coaching, and least of all in the mode of teaching that is Socratic, which is sometimes called "maieutic." That Greek word signifies midwifery—bringing (ideas) to birth.

The midwife does not produce the offspring; she merely helps the mother to give birth. Most of the effort and all of the pain of the labor are experienced by the mother. The midwife makes the mother's effort easier and also, perhaps, less painful. Both mother and midwife take joy in what they together have brought forth.

Didactic teaching, no less than coaching and Socratic teaching, only helps or assists in the process of learning, making it easier, less painful, more productive. Improvement of the mind,

23

in all three lines of learning, always results primarily from the activity of the learner's own mind, and only secondarily from the assistance afforded by the teacher in the process.

When the teacher tries to play the primary role of imparting knowledge, passively received and without its being understood, only the student's memory is affected, not his or her mind. Examinations are passed by regurgitation of what is remembered from lectures and textbooks. Most of the remembered information is subsequently forgotten; and the student's mind at the end of the process is no better than it was at the beginning.

(3) The learning that should be done cannot all take place during school hours. Schooling must include homework, in increasing amounts from grade to grade. Moreover, the homework done must be examined by the teachers if the students are to take the assignments seriously and fulfill them conscientiously.

(4) The consideration of homework leads us, finally, to the role that parents must play in their children's schooling. The obligations of parenting are not discharged by simply sending children to school. Parents who do not monitor the doing of homework, who do not provide an environment conducive to doing it, who do not encourage the doing of more of it rather than less, are derelict in their educational duty as parents.

They are also derelict if they do not support the authority of teachers, and especially of principals, with regard to good behavior. Rules of deportment—quietness, docility, mutual respect between teachers and students—must be enforced if the school is to be a place where teaching and learning can occur effectively.

4
Questions About the Principles

(1) *The Range of Questions*

IN THE TWELVE MONTHS before the publication of *The Paideia Proposal*, what were to become its central theses had become sufficiently clear to enable the Chairman and other members of the Paideia Group to present summaries of them to a variety of educational groups and organizations. In the twelve months since the book was published, it has had a nationwide circulation that generated invitations to members of the Paideia Group to discuss the proposed educational reform or to attend educational conferences at which it was made the subject of discussion.

All these encounters have been occasions for the raising of questions and for attempts to answer them. Reviews of the book have been another source of questions to be considered. Still another source has been interviews conducted on television and radio.*

Against this background of experience, we are in a position to survey the questions asked and to present considered responses to them. It will be seen that the questions are not all

---

*See Appendix I for a list of these encounters and interviews and also for a list of critical notices, reviews, and other comments, unfavorable as well as favorable.

of the same kind, not on the same plane of discourse about the educational problems to be solved.

This chapter will deal only with those questions that concern the Paideia principles. Under this head we have questions about the objectives to be aimed at and questions about the general means for attaining them; and a few other questions that have some bearing on these matters. Problems of implementation will be reserved for the chapter to follow.

The questions treated here have been raised by educational administrators, school boards or boards of education, associations of principals or of teachers, and other educational groups across the country, as well as by participants in the various encounters mentioned above and listed in Appendix I.

These questions fall into four groups: first, questions about the recommended curricular framework; second, questions about the applicability of the course of study to all students and their reaction to it; third, questions about teachers and teaching; and, finally, questions about matters of organization, administration, and financing.

As we said a moment ago, only the first set of questions will be dealt with at length in this chapter. They are the ones that go to the heart of the matter and that must be given satisfactory answers; otherwise all else becomes irrelevant.

With regard to the questions in the other three sets, it is often difficult to draw a line that sharply separates an interest in the essence of the program itself from concerns or perplexities about how to implement it in this or that particular detail. It will therefore be convenient to answer some of these questions summarily here and return to them in the next chapter.

(2) *Questions About the Recommended Curricular Framework*

QUESTION 1: *Is not* The Paideia Proposal *just another form of the "back to basics" movement?*

ANSWER: Yes and no, depending on the scope given the word "basics." If you use that word narrowly, as many do, to refer only to the so-called three R's, then the answer is emphatically negative, as anyone who examines the curricular framework can see for himself. The kind of learning and teaching that can be accomplished only in seminar discussions of books and other works of art and that requires teachers to employ the Socratic method of questioning is not contemplated at all in the customary appeal for a return to basics; nor does the customary appeal envisage the scope of instruction and learning here proposed with regard to the basic fields of subject-matter.

If however, the word "basics" is interpreted broadly enough to cover everything that should be included in the stage of schooling that is basic because it underlies all other schooling and learning, then *The Paideia Proposal* can be associated with the "back to basics" movement.

In its insistence on restoring or increasing the kind of teaching that is coaching, without which the basic intellectual skills of reading, writing, speaking, listening, of mathematical operations and of scientific procedures cannot be developed, the proposal has a close affinity with the "back to basics" movement—certainly to the extent that its supporters advocate such skills. Such teaching and learning once existed for the few and must now be restored and made available to all.

As to other elements in the Paideia program that are also "basic" in our sense, to think of them as a return to something that once existed in our schools is wide of the mark.

27

QUESTION 2: *Does not* The Paideia Proposal *amount to little more than a call for the restoration of a classical education, its only novelty being that it advocates giving such an education to all the children instead of only to some—the college-bound?*

ANSWER: Here again the answer could be both yes and no, though it must be more negative than affirmative.

The term "classical" has a number of connotations, most of which do not apply at all to the Paideia proposal. If it means an educational program that prescribes and relies heavily on the study of Greek and Latin and on works written in these languages, then it does not apply at all. If it means an educational program that demands an almost exclusive concentration on the great books, then, too, it does not apply.

When the word "classical" is used, in a very loose sense, to refer to elements that once existed in our educational tradition, it becomes almost synonymous in meaning with the word "traditional." Then there is ground for viewing the Paideia proposal as harking back to something traditional—but only in part. There are innovations in the Paideia recommendations that have no precedent in anything that comprised "classical" or "traditional" education. It is quite misleading to identify the reading of some great books—or, for that matter, any discussable books that are not textbooks (which are obviously undiscussable)—as a return to the classics.

The word "classic" (which can, of course, mean anything of lasting value) too often means *only* the works of antiquity, to be studied *only* for their antiquarian interest, not for their relevance to the contemporary world.

The Paideia program recommends the reading and discussion of classics—that is, any works of lasting value—only in the sense that the books and other artifacts chosen have this lasting value and only for the sake of their relevance to problems that anyone must face in today's world.

QUESTION 3: *There is much talk today about strengthening the humanities in our schools. Is* The Paideia Proposal *an effort to do just that?*

ANSWER: Like the term "basics" and the term "classics," the term "humanities" is much misused, because taken too narrowly in current discussions. In its current use, it stands for certain subject-matters, such as literature and other fine arts, and sometimes for history, as against the subject-matters of mathematics and the sciences, natural and social.

Anyone who glances at the recommended curricular framework will see at once that *The Paideia Proposal* places as much emphasis on mathematics and on the sciences as on history, literature, and other fine arts.

What is even more important for those who ask this question to understand is that the word "humanities" has a meaning now almost totally lost from view in current educational discussion. If they will turn to the dedication page of this book, they will find that the Latin word "humanitas" is equivalent in meaning to the Greek word "paideia," its acquired significance being the *general* learning that should be the possession of every human being.

In this meaning of the term, we should not speak of the humanities as a set of special (non-scientific) subject-matters. We should rather speak of a humanistic, which is to say a *generalist,* approach to the study of any subject-matter, scientific as well as non-scientific.

29

Throughout *The Paideia Proposal,* we never use the word "humanities" in its twentieth-century sense to denote a set of subjects to be studied. We always speak of an educational program that is general, not specialized; that is liberal, not vocational; and that is humanistic, not technical. We might go even further and say that it cannot be general and liberal without being humanistic, or humanistic without being liberal and general.

The Paideia Proposal does not call for "strengthening" the "humanities" as one set of subjects as against other subjects, equally important for general learning as an element in the curriculum. It calls for a course of study that is humanistic *throughout*—generalist, not specialist, in its approach to the study of anything.

QUESTION 4: *Is not* The Paideia Proposal *implicitly, if not overtly, elitist in its recommendations?*

ANSWER: Nothing could be further from the truth! In page after page, chapter after chapter, *The Paideia Proposal* repeats that what it recommends is intended for *all* children in any and every school, and along a single track. Two-track or multi-track programs, or programs that sharply distinguish the college-bound from those for whom basic schooling is terminal, may be called elitist, and such elitism exists in the public school system at present.

The Paideia program is a one-track program. It allows for no differentiation whatever between the college-bound and the rest. It maintains that all children are truly educable and educable in precisely the same sense of that word. It explicitly rejects the elitist view that only some are innately well enough endowed to be educable, while the rest can only be trained for routine jobs, not prepared for the duties of citizenship and not prepared for continued learning in adult life, regardless of college.

The elitist, explicitly or implicitly, views the human race as divided into two classes—the educable and the non-educable (equivalent to Aristotle's freemen by nature and slaves by nature). If the elitist had the courage of his convictions, he would recommend the abandonment of universal suffrage and, with it, a retreat from our democratic institutions.

How, then, are we to understand the perversity of the question whether our proposal is elitist? Only in this way: where the word "elitist" is used to mean a concern with excellence, then the Paideia program—a program designed to provide a high quality of schooling—can be labelled "elitist," but only when it is also understood that its "elitism" is applicable to all, not just a privileged few. It is concerned with excellence as a democratic goal. The word "elitist" thus amounts to no more than name-calling.

QUESTION 5: The Paideia Proposal *reiterates that little word "all" and stresses it by adding "all without exception." Is this merely for rhetorical effect? Do the members of the Paideia Group really believe that what they are advocating is applicable to all—all without exception? If so, how can they persuade those of us who have grave doubts about the soundness of their belief?*

ANSWER: In the first place, when we use the word "all," we are referring to all who go to school and remain there. And when we say "all without exception," we are not overlooking the fact that some of the children in our schools may need special help to overcome recognized learning disabilities.

31

In the second place, when we claim that the Paideia program, if adopted for all, will accomplish the goals aimed at for all, we do not mean that all will achieve that result to the same degree. Individual differences in degree among the children with regard to their capacity for learning (or, in other words, individual differences in the degree of their educability) will lead to differences in degree in the end result, but differences in *degree,* not differences in *kind.*

If containers differing in their capacity, ranging from half-pint containers up to gallon containers, are all filled to the brim, they are all equally full, for each is full up to its initial capacity. But if some of the containers, those that are least capacious, are filled to the brim with water; if some, slightly more capacious, are filled with skimmed milk; if some still more capacious are filled with whole milk; and if only the largest containers are filled with rich cream, then their being thus filled to the brim results in a difference in *kind,* not just in *degree.*

Our position is that all the containers, differing in degree of capacity, should not only end up being filled to the brim, but that all should also be filled with the same substance—with a half-pint of cream in the half-pint container and a gallon of cream in the gallon container.

In the third place, though it is proper and reasonable to challenge our contention that the Paideia program is applicable to all without exception, it is so only if that challenge is intended to make the point that we do not yet know precisely how to do what should be done, and not if the point is that it cannot be done at all.

We are prepared to concede that, with the best efforts conceivable, we may never be able to achieve one hundred percent success. That may always remain an unattainable desideratum, as is the case in almost all human endeavors. It runs counter to all experience to suppose that ideals are ever fully attainable.

But we also know that unless we strive for the fullest achievement of the goals we aim at, it is unlikely that we shall ever get close to them. Unless we persevere in aiming at success with *all*, we will never make progress toward closing the gap between success and failure. On the contrary, if we adopt the mood of hopelessness and yield to counsels of despair, we will probably end up doing what should be done with a percentage of the whole much smaller than the percentage that is actually attainable.

Those who challenge our hopes and are willing to settle for what is easily doable are, by that very fact, settling for a goal that they themselves set too low and keep too low. They have resigned themselves to shortchanging a considerable percentage of the children.

Complete success will always elude us, but substantial progress toward that unattainable goal will certainly not be made unless we persevere with patience in a sustained effort over at least a generation—twenty or thirty years, or more. The reform of basic schooling—or any other institution—is not something to be accomplished overnight or even in a decade or two.

QUESTION 6: *There are many reform movements today that demand that the quality of education in our public schools be improved. Is the Paideia Group's efforts to be identified with one of these?*

ANSWER: Certainly, *The Paideia Proposal* calls for a much higher quality of schooling than any that now exists in our

33

public schools; and it sets up much higher standards of accomplishment for that higher quality of instruction.

At the same time, it differs in two significant respects from almost all the other reform movements now calling for improved quality: first, it insists that the quality be improved for all; second, it insists that the improvement in quality occur *through the whole twelve years of basic schooling,* not just in the first eight or last four years. It is not the lower schools or the high schools that are to be rescued by ad hoc methods. It is the whole scheme of basic schooling that must be re-thought and re-built.

QUESTION #7: *You say that your required course of study should be the same for all the children in school? Does this mean that you are calling for the elimination of the special education programs that now exist?*

ANSWER: The special education programs that now exist fall into two groups: (1) programs intended for those with special learning disabilities; (2) programs intended for specially gifted children.

It is plain that this division between two types of special education is not symmetrical. The first deals with a clear problem; not so the second. Our answer accordingly is that we recommend the abandonment of the second and the retention of the first.

The greatly improved quality of the Paideia curriculum makes special programs for the specially gifted totally unnecessary. Such programs are doubtless needed now because existing courses of study, instruction, and standards are so poor in quality and so deficient in content that the specially gifted suffer deprivation. But the Paideia program will give the specially

34

gifted every opportunity to use their talents to the fullest measure. There is, therefore, no need to retain special programs for them.

If the specially gifted have surplus energy and avidity for learning after they have done their best in the required studies, this surplus can be used by having them learn more by teaching their less able classmates.

On the other hand, those with special learning disabilities do need special help, and programs should be devised to help them to become satisfactory achievers in a course of study that is the same for all. As it happens, it is in such special education programs now in force that we find the kind of coaching which should also be present in the schooling of those who do not have learning disabilities.

These existing programs of special education exemplify what *The Paideia Proposal* means by supplementary instruction. The help given individual students in these programs should, in the Paideia scheme, be available to any student who is falling behind or who starts with learning deficiences that are not due to pathological deficiencies or disabilities.

QUESTION 8: The Paideia Proposal *calls for the elimination of all electives, except the choice of a second language, the study of which is itself required. Will this not stultify the individuality of individually different students, with different interests, propensities, or talents? Will this not work hardship on the specially gifted, who should be allowed to make the most of their special gifts? And is not your elimination of electives an authoritarian infringement on individual liberty and freedom of choice?*

ANSWER: First of all, the reason for the elimination of all electives is that, if the indispensable elements in the prescribed curricular framework are to be well-learned and well-taught, there is no time for anything else. Many of the electives thereby eliminated have no educational value at all; some have a value that can be realized in one or another form of extracurricular activity.

Second, neither regimentation nor deprivation result from the same required course of study for all. The notion that a common curriculum will shape the young into so many identical cookies punched out by the same cookie-cutter is contrary to all experience. Those of us who have taught students in required courses know that individuals react to such instruction differently according to their individuality. That is what individuality means. It is not warped or crushed by a common fare, either mental or physical. Indeed, the more facility students have with the basic skills, the more their minds are filled with knowledge and are engaged in sustained discussion, the more each will strengthen his inner self and develop along individual lines.

Individual differences simply cannot be repressed. Different individuals react differently to reading the same newspapers and magazines, watching the same television shows, going to the same plays or sporting events. Likewise, individually different students will respond differently to the impact upon them of the same required course of study. Their interests, propensities, and talents will come out correspondingly different.

Third, a completely required course of study humanistically conceived might perhaps work hardship in the case of the rare genius—in mathematics, music, dance, or some other art—who cannot be restrained from intense specialization at a very early age. Allowing or encouraging such intense specialization in childhood may, of course, result in regrettable intellectual and human imbalances. That may be the price one has to pay for being a genius. But no plan for the reform of basic schooling for 60 million children should be criticized for its failure to provide for geniuses.

The great merit in eliminating the present plethora of electives is that it will keep students from wasting their time in courses that are of low instructional value and that fit in no coherent scheme of progressive learning.

Fourth, we must warn against the mistake of interpreting the curricular framework delineated in the diagram on page 18 as if it were a fully determined course of study in which the arrangement and specification of all the components are laid down for every school in the country. We have tried to make the point clear. We must repeat once again: it is only a framework of ends and of general means that is prescribed.

Finally, the charge that a required course of study is authoritarian and anti-democratic is groundless. One might just as well say that requiring children to be vaccinated or otherwise rendered immune, or requiring them to have balanced diets, take a certain amount of physical exercise, have a certain amount of sleep at regular intervals, and submit to medications they need for the cure of ailments they suffer, is authoritarian and anti-democratic. At a higher level, the requirements for a job or for a profession are and will remain uniform without being on that account any infringement of liberty. There is plenty of room left for the exercise of freedom of choice in other matters.

The positive point to remember is that to become an educated person one must be both a generalist and a specialist—a generalist to begin with and a specialist afterwards. One cannot become a competent specialist without exercising freedom of choice that expresses one's individual interests, propensities, and gifts. It is equally true that one cannot become a generalist by insisting upon freedom of choice to indulge one's individual interests, propensities, and gifts.

QUESTION 9: *In a Paideia school, what will happen to the extracurricular activities so prevalent and so preoccupying in today's secondary schools? Specifically, what role do you see for student activity on debating teams, school newspapers, and in athletic events?*

ANSWER: We acknowledge that all these activities have some educational merit. Debating is a good exercise in putting together and expressing coherent arguments. Both writing and business acumen can be sharpened by work on a school newspaper. In addition to physical fitness and skill, athletics, if well supervised, can develop traits of character, such as self-discipline, stamina, personal courage, and team spirit. On these grounds, such activities can serve as supplements and reinforcements in a Paideia program.

But we must draw a line, thin as it may be, between the prescribed Paideia experience during the school day—mornings and early afternoons—and any of these optional extracurricular activities scheduled later on in the day. The latter, we insist, must not be permitted to encroach on the priority and scheduling of the former. The same goes for financial resources; they should not be diverted from the serious business of schooling to the support of these supplementary activities.

QUESTION 10: *You say you are not prescribing a rigid curriculum, that you allow for differences between schools and among different school districts. At the same time, you insist not only upon a required course of study, but you indicate subject-*

matters such as history, mathematics, biology, and so forth which you obviously think cannot be left out of any school anywhere. Is this not contradictory, not to say disingenuous, on your part?

ANSWER: There is a difference between saying that certain subject-matters should be covered and certain skills acquired, on the one hand, and on the other hand, that they should be presented in a given order, in a specific manner, with an identical content, or to a fixed degree.

The Paideia Proposal, in stipulating history, does expect that this will be taught in every school. It further assumes that in every school the history taught will to some extent be that of Europe as well as of the United States, since it is from Europe that the country's basic institutions and its prevailing culture derive. But we do not say at what point in the child's schooling this study should come, for how long it should go on, and still less what syllabi or textbooks should be used to teach it. Varieties of approach and emphasis are to be expected, as are differences of interpretation.

The Paideia Proposal likewise assumes that mathematics will be taught in every school, and even stipulates that a stated degree of proficiency—through the calculus—shall be acquired by every student. But again, there is no stipulation in the proposal as to the organization of mathematical study in time or substance. Far from assuming the usual progression from arithmetic through algebra, geometry, and trigonometry to calculus, the Paideia Group allows, and even hopes, that different and quite innovative approaches will be tried. Hardly any subject is more in need of fresh presentation than mathematics in the schools, and there is every expectation and every encouragement in the proposal that this will happen. The same thing can be said about the sciences such as physics, biology, and chemistry. These can be kept distinct or integrated, or put in sequence or combination, according to differing plans.

In Column Two studies, where the concern is with the coaching and the development of skills, proficiency is called for in such linguistic skills as reading, writing, speaking, listening, and also in all the skills of mathematical and scientific operations, including what is now called computer literacy; but again, the timing and arrangement of these things will vary and can be kept flexible to suit different circumstances.

The proposal assumes that there is no stage of basic schooling where the need for practice in *all* these skills does not exist. Hence, practice should go on throughout the twelve years of basic schooling, but just as it may begin with rhythmic exercises in kindergarten, so it may end with laboratory experiments and training in computer programming in the upper grades.

Finally, in Column Three, the proposal assumes that interesting and worthwhile materials—books, paintings, music, films, and the like—will be discussed by children of all ages, but we offer no list of works that must be taken up, nor any sequence in their use. We may have suggestions to make about these materials in a forthcoming book entitled *The Paideia Program,* but they are *only* suggestions—illustrations of what can be done.

QUESTION 11: *You have mentioned computer literacy among the skills to be developed in Paideia schools. What position does the Paideia Group take on the new technologies?*

ANSWER: We embrace them. Computers will soon be in most places of work and in many homes. They should, therefore, be present in all schools and in many classrooms.

Computers have shown themselves to be effective tools in facilitating Column Two learning. Computer-assisted teaching, when competently conducted, can be an excellent and cost-effective way of delivering the kind of coaching and drill that is indispensable for the development of the intellectual skills. As the price of computers falls, we can anticipate a time when every student will have his or her own individual mechanical "coach." This will help to make economically feasible the small student-teacher ratio needed for Column Two learning. Moreover, foreign language teaching can be materially aided by the use of tape recording, though, again, the language laboratory must be competently set up and supervised.

Technology will also play an important role in Column One teaching and learning. It is a rare teacher who can give an effective and arresting performance as a lecturer. Why not, then, periodically use video tapes of the best lectures available on every subject to be taught didactically in Column One? The classroom teacher is then free to concentrate on questions, discussions, and on individual instruction where needed.

Column Three is the one place where technology can help little, if at all. The discussion of ideas and values, based on the reading of important books and on the experience of other works of art, is the least mechanical of all human operations and thus least susceptible to mechanical facilitation.

Endorsing the educational use of technological devices of every kind does not mean that we approve of their use in basic schooling in order to train students for careers as computer programmers, as computer technicians, or for any other narrowly vocational purpose. In approving the use of computers or other devices, we are not abandoning our opposition to particularized job training of every sort.

41

QUESTION 12: *Does* The Paideia Proposal's *elimination of all particularized job training from the prescribed course of study mean that it calls for the dismantling of our vocational high schools? Does the Paideia Group think that vocational training, in the sense of specialized training for this or that line of work, is without value? Is there no need to help the young prepare to earn a living?*

ANSWER: To the first of these three questions, we reply by expressing the hope that many of the students who have had a Paideia schooling for the first eight years will not elect to go to vocational high schools. We cannot estimate in advance what the effect of the first eight years will be. There is no reason, therefore, to call for the dismantling of vocational high schools. They will survive or dwindle according to the effect on the young of eight years of Paideia schooling.

After twelve years of general and liberal schooling has been completed, some of the graduates of Paideia schools will want technical training of one sort or another to fit them for special jobs, in which to earn a living. Such training should be available to them in public institutions. Such further schooling is now in part offered in most four-year colleges and in almost all community two-year colleges.

To the second question, our answer is that with the rapidity of technological advances and with the increasing role of robots and computers in the production of both goods and services, narrowly specialized job training in schools will become less and less useful. It will not fit the jobs available. Retraining will have to take place on the job more often than not. Almost always the only form of adequate training will have to be on the job, not in school.

42

It should further be observed that vocational training at the secondary level of the kind that prepares students for a narrowly particular sort of work has about it something undemocratic. By focusing on one particular sort of job, it minimizes their opportunities and hinders them from advancing beyond such work. It deprives students of the flexibility needed to adjust to a changing job market, more and more rapidly affected by technological advances.

What *The Paideia Proposal* has to say about preparation for earning a living constitutes our answer to the third question. We have declared that earning a living is one of the three main objectives of basic schooling.

Preparation for earning a living is served in two ways. First, it is served by the development of intellectual skills, all of which are skills of learning. The graduate of a Paideia school will have the trained intelligence to adjust and adapt. They will know how to acquire new skills quickly and how to perform well the new tasks they are assigned.

To recognize this is to recognize that a completely general and liberal schooling is the most practical and useful preparation for earning a living in the job market of the future. Learning one kind of job ahead of time in school may once have been the best form of preparation for earning a living. It is no longer.

Second, it should be remembered that the Paideia curricular framework includes one or two years devoted to a general introduction to the world of work. This means a survey of existing lines of employment and of the talents needed to succeed in them. Its inclusion indicates no lack of positive interest on our part in the preparation of the young for earning a living.

43

Whatever technical or professional preparation for earning a living requires additional schooling, instead of training on the job itself, should be available for all in collegiate institutions or in universities, in special technical institutes or research agencies.

The more the Paideia reform succeeds, the more Paideia schools come into existence, the more their graduates will go on to such advanced institutions—some for the purpose of preparing themselves for life-long self-education; some also for the business of earning a living.

QUESTION 13: *At what age should Paideia schooling begin and how long should it last?*

ANSWER: For some children it can begin as early as the age of four. It should begin for all no later than at the age of six. On the average, it should last twelve years; but some children may complete basic schooling in ten or eleven years; others may take thirteen or fourteen.

QUESTION 14: *What is the position of the Paideia Group with regard to state-mandated courses, such as state history, personal hygiene, driver education, or sex education?*

ANSWER: To some extent, certain state-mandated "learning" can be accommodated within the Paideia framework. For example, the basic elements of personal hygiene can be incorporated in the early grades, and some of the elements of sex-education can be covered during the study of the biological sciences. Anything beyond that? It is our position that the school cannot and should not take over what has traditionally been the responsibility of families, churches, and other institutions charged with the well-being of youth.

As for driver-education, it is our position that this is also the responsibility of the parent or guardian. In practice, this responsibility has been abdicated and has quite unreasonably been unloaded on the schools.

That "tradition" is now too strong to shrug off. Driver education will have to be handled as an aspect of manual training, along with machine repair, carpentry, cooking and sewing, typing and shorthand.

As for state history, the case for its inclusion continues to weaken as we become a nation of internal migrants. Still, state requirements can be satisfied by including state history in that part of the curriculum devoted to history, geography, and the study of social institutions.

It should be stressed that Paideia sets its face against the process by which a "problem" is identified, turned into a "subject," and then inserted into the school curriculum for its solution. Drug abuse, unsafe driving, and the defrauding of consumers are doubtless serious matters but it is unfair and unwise to designate the schoolroom as the one place where these things are dealt with. If the school is made the repository of every social concern, education itself is bound to be crowded out—and the social problems will remain. More is less!

QUESTION 15: *What about state-mandated competency standards?*

ANSWER: A student who does what is required in the Paideia program should have no difficulty at all in handling the current crop of competency tests. Some of these tests are poorly conceived and constructed; they mainly reward the recollection of disconnected items of information, rather than call for the possession of organized and well-understood bodies of knowledge.

45

The Paideia program does not underestimate the importance of memorization and recall, but never as an end in itself, only as a highly useful support for genuine intellectual processes. Any test that measures only rote memory will not test the achievement of Paideia students.

QUESTION 16: *How does the Paideia program take care of civics and the formation of moral character? Neither of these things appears to be mentioned as part of the required course of study.*

ANSWER: They are not explicitly mentioned, but they are most certainly there.

The Paideia program regards civics, or preparation for citizenship by knowledge and understanding of the institutions of this country, as the second of the three main objectives of basic schooling. Its curricular requirements provide such preparation in two ways. One is through didactic instruction in history and the growth of social institutions, a comparative study of which will include and emphasize the institutions of our own country.

The other is more direct and is so important as to make shocking its almost total absence from basic schooling as it now exists. *The Paideia Proposal* explicitly recommends seminars in which students read and discuss the Declaration of Independence, the Constitution of the United States, the *Federalist Papers* by Hamilton, Madison, and Jay, *Democracy in America* by Alexis de Tocqueville, and Lincoln's Gettysburg Address. In such seminars, the students' understanding of such ideas as liberty, equality, justice, rights, property, constitutional government, citizenship, and democracy will be enlarged and clarified. What could be better education in civics than this? What better preparation for citizenship in our constitutional democracy?

As for the formation of moral character, there is, first of all, the Paideia insistence that a well-run school must enforce standards of behavior conducive to learning. Second, the portion of the Paideia program that is devoted to the enlargment of the understanding of basic ideas and values involves the discussion of moral problems and will deal with the ideas and values that are involved in facing such problems.

While understanding by itself does not guarantee the formation of a good moral character, it does contribute to that result by making students defend the value judgments they make and by getting them to realize the consequences of holding sound ideas about such matters.

QUESTION 17: *Your educational manifesto mentions only public schools. Does it apply equally to private or independent schools, both parochial and other?*

ANSWER: Yes, most emphatically, because of their greater independence and autonomy. It should be much easier for private or independent schools to adopt the Paideia recommendations. Such schools, by undertaking experiments and providing models, may even help the public school system to move in the same direction.

QUESTION 18: The Paideia Proposal *sets before us an ideal for basic schooling in a democratic society. No one committed to the principles of democracy can dissent from Paideia's commitment to the principle of equal educational opportunity—equal in quality as well as in quantity.*

Paideia recognizes that something must be done to overcome individual inequalities—especially those stemming from differ-

47

ences in native endowment and from differences in nurtural background. It suggests pre-school tutoring to overcome such disadvantages as well as supplemental instruction for those who need help along the way.

Even supposing that these remedies for the disadvantaged are both feasible and adequate, The Paideia Proposal *fails to recognize the grave social and economic inequalities that still prevail in our society, especially the absence of an equality of economic opportunity that confronts a substantial portion of schoolchildren. Is it not whistling in the dark, or just making empty gestures toward an ideal, to suppose that an effort to establish equality of educational opportunity can succeed before our society has first succeeded in equalizing social and economic opportunity and conditions?*

ANSWER: *The Paideia Proposal* was not silent on this point. In Chapter 11, it explicitly addressed itself to the problem.

A basic human right is the right to obtain a decent livelihood by working for it under decent conditions. Those whom the economy leaves unemployed through no fault of their own are unjustly deprived of an essential human right which is indispensable to their pursuit of happiness.

As things stand now, that part of the school population which comes from severely disadvantaged minorities can look forward to unemployment after school—thrown on the waste heap of a society that is squandering its human resources. Hopelessness about the future is bound to affect motivation in school. Why do the hard work that good basic schooling would demand if, after doing it, no opportunity exists to work for a decent living? This bleak prospect makes for the dropout, or, what is just as bad, turns the energetic into the delinquent. While still in school, they regard themselves as prisoners serving time.

48

The Paideia Proposal calls for an educational revolution—a change in public schooling that is indispensable to the fulfillment of the ideals of a truly democratic society. We are aware that that revolution cannot be fully accomplished without its being accompanied by social and economic changes in the same direction.

The two sets of changes—the educational changes on the one hand and the social and economic changes on the other—must go forward together and interact with one another. We cannot wait for the social and economic improvements to be fully accomplished before we start on efforts to bring about the necessary educational changes. Each set of changes needs the support of the other.

We anticipate that more and more students who have completed the Paideia program will go on to advanced schooling instead of going immediately to work. This, we think, will be especially true of students coming from lower income groups.

It seems appropriate to add here that students who go on to colleges and graduate schools after having completed twelve years of Paideia schooling will be a very different breed from the kind that now apply for admission to our institutions of higher learning. This will inevitably alter for the better the character of these institutions. It will enable colleges to do what they should be doing now but cannot, because of the deficiencies in basic schooling they are compelled to remedy. It will also improve the technical and professional preparation that these higher institutions provide.

QUESTION 19: The Paideia Proposal *and its advocates speak again and again about raising the quality of basic schooling for all the children. This is vain and empty talk unless well-*

49

defined standards of accomplishment in all phases or aspects of the Paideia program are shown to be clearly higher than those now set for graduation at the end of twelve years of basic schooling.

How does the Paideia Group define the minimum standards of accomplishment for graduation in each of the three types of learning that it insists upon as ingredients of basic schooling?

What sort of tests, examinations, or other measures are to be used for determining whether students have met the minimum standards? How do these Paideia standards and measurements support your claim that a Paideia schooling will be of much higher quality than any that now exists?

ANSWER: This question cannot be fully answered here. Anything like a comprehensive answer can be given only after the Paideia Group has completed work in process. That work consists in describing in detail each of the elements set forth in the curricular framework delineated in the diagram on page 18.

These descriptions will make up *The Paideia Program,* a third book to be published in the coming year. It will consist of a series of essays by members of the Paideia Group, each dealing with one of the major elements in the curricular framework— the subject-matters to be taught didactically in Column One, the skills to be developed by coaching in Column Two, and the enhancement of the understanding of basic ideas and values to be achieved by the Socratically conducted seminars of Column Three.

In advance of that more comprehensive statement, we can do no more than offer a few preliminary and tentative observations.

50

We think Paideia students should at least be able to meet the standards set in other technologically advanced countries—in mathematics and natural science, in history and social studies, and in the skills of reading and writing.

They should be expected to meet standards much, much higher than those now accepted for high school graduation, though not all students can be expected to meet standards as high as those now set in advanced placement tests.

Most should do much better than the present average all along the line, and at the same time they should do much more, for the following reasons: (1) reading and writing will not be the only intellectual skills developed; (2) achievement in mathematics will go as far as the calculus; (3) the study of the natural sciences will include physics; (4) the study of history will be deepened and enlarged; and (5), most important of all, an understanding of basic ideas and values will be included in any measurement of Paideia accomplishments. These will be tested (among other ways) by a student's ability to construct an oral defense of an opinion he or she has advanced, and of his or her ability to participate in the discussion of basic issues or problems. Student accomplishment will also include facility in at least two languages—English and one other language.

With regard to skills, a Paideia graduate should be able to show an understanding of a moderately complicated essay; an ability to write clear and concise expository prose, to perform reasonably complicated mathematical operations, to sort out issues, to solve various types of problems, to think through an argument and evaluate it, to formulate a persuasive argument and deliver it orally, to listen critically to a speech and respond relevantly to it.

All Paideia graduates, we hope, will have read with understanding the Declaration of Independence, the Constitution of the United States, the *Federalist Papers, Democracy in America,* and The Gettysburg Address—these documents being the groundwork of preparation for citizenship.

A tall order, indeed, when we remember that many of our seventeen and eighteen year olds are today indisposed to using their minds and incapable of using them in any sustained process of thought. Nothing has shown that they are naturally incapable or naturally uninterested. Rather their native mental powers have been left untrained and unchallenged. The difficulty is not with the students but with a society that has expected too little of them and has not managed to equip teachers or students for the task they face. The standards suggested by Paideia are far from impossible of attainment. But they must be worked for if they are to be attained.

Written tests and other modes of examination, used for measuring accomplishment, must shift their focus from emphasis on verbal memory and the guesswork that is encouraged by true-false and multiple choice tests, to an emphasis on the possession of organized knowledge (not just bits of information), on demonstrable linguistic and mathematical skills; and on the power to understand, think, and communicate.

Intellectual skills, including those of thinking and understanding, cannot be assessed by machine-graded tests. Essays must be written and must be read by teachers. Writing must be taught and tested by teachers who themselves can write well. Mathematical reasoning must be tracked. Thinking and understanding require oral examinations among other tests.

Is all this utopian? Not if it follows hard upon sound schooling and competent teaching; not if school authorities realize that evaluation is a complicated process, not be done hastily or on the cheap.

The aforestated standards are routinely met by some American and many foreign students. The question lingers: *Why not by all?*

(3) *Questions About the Applicability of the Program to Students and Their Reaction to It*

QUESTION 20: *Does the Paideia plan apply to younger children—children in the first six grades? It would appear to be much more applicable to high school students or at most to those from grade seven up. Is that the case?*

ANSWER: The Paideia plan has, from the very outset, been conceived as a plan for all twelve years of basic schooling, not just for high schools or the upper six years. In our view, no permanent reform of secondary education can be accomplished without making the elementary level, from grade one up, effective and truly preparatory.

Our distinction among the three modes of learning and teaching is as applicable to very young children in the first grade as to seniors in high school. That differentiation does not call for departmentalization in the lower grades. On the contrary, as we have repeatedly said, the three modes of learning and of teaching must be integrated at all levels. The traditional self-contained primary school classroom is closer to our ideal than the fractionalized, departmentalized high school program.

Departmentalization may be required for didactic instruction in such subjects as mathematics, the natural sciences, history, and foreign languages. When students reach a certain level of difficulty in what is to be learned, departmentalization becomes useful. But it is not now required at the elementary levels of didactic instruction, and the Paideia plan calls for no change in that respect.

What does and can happen in the elementary classroom, where all the phases of learning occur in relation to one another, must be made to happen at the upper levels as well, though it may be more difficult to achieve there.

QUESTION 21: *Will the Paideia program hold the interest of students? Can they be motivated to do the kind of work it calls for? If they are not given training for particular jobs by which to earn a living, will not many of them drop out of school? If, for that reason or any other, they lack interest and motivation, how can discipline be maintained?*

ANSWER: One of the reasons why we think that the Paideia program must be initiated in the lower grades—from grades one on up—is that it will be much easier for students to do the things the Paideia program calls for at the very start of their schooling. Young people whose minds have not been engaged in the pursuit of learning from the very outset of schooling are much more difficult to interest and motivate later on.

The natural curiosity of the very young, their innate propensity for learning, if properly handled in the early grades, will turn them into *students*. Their interest and motivation will grow with the years.

There is nothing about the Paideia program that generates new problems of arousing interest and motivating study. On the contrary, such difficulties arise now because the existing course of study and the predominant mode of teaching fail to engage the students' minds, fail to give them a sense of accomplishment, reduce them to passive recipients, compelled to memorize instead of being active learners, and, above all, do not challenge them sufficiently, leaving them bored and craving outlets for unused energy.

It may be thought that our concern with enlarging the understanding of basic ideas and values introduces matters that are too abstract or too remote from the lives and interests of the very young and also of contemporary teenagers. That is not the case.

The questions that very young children are prone to ask—"why" questions for the most part—manifest their innate urge to seek understanding, not merely information. Questions about ideas and values are not foreign to them. When dealt with by teachers skilled in carrying on discussions, they are neither too abstract nor too remote for the young.

QUESTION 22: *How does the Paideia program deal with the non-academic interests of the students—their social life, their games and sports, their outside activities?*

ANSWER: The Paideia program leaves as much time for other legitimate interests as existing programs do. As we pointed out earlier, many extracurricular activities can be encouraged and provided for in a Paideia school to the same extent that they are now. Play of all sorts is not only fun; it is also therapeutic, affording relaxation and recreation that renews energy for academic work.

The social activities of students in Paideia schools, far from being suppressed or side-tracked, can be enlivened and enlightened by the sharper and stronger consciousness engendered by the program.

(4) *Questions About Teachers and Teaching*

QUESTION 23: *Clearly, the success of the Paideia program depends upon the number of good teachers available. They appear to be in short supply. Can we find enough teachers competent to teach calculus and physics? May not this fact militate against putting the Paideia proposal into practice?*

ANSWER: The question is prompted by a dubious statement of fact.

It is true that *The Paideia Proposal* depends a great deal on effective teaching in all phases of the curriculum; in Chapter 7, it declares that the quality of the teaching will determine the quality of the learning. That is the "heart of the matter."

It is not true, however, that the number of able teachers available is too small for an effective initiation of the Paideia program. If they are given an opportunity to work under proper conditions, and if their talents and skills are employed for the guidance—in effect, the coaching—of less able teachers, the level of teaching in a school can be raised to the requisite quality.

This is not to say that, with the Paideia reform in mind, the training of teachers in the future cannot be greatly improved. Chapter 7 of *The Paideia Proposal* outlines recommendations for doing just that. But such future improvements in the training of teachers, especially for coaching and for the Socratic method of teaching, need not be awaited before initial steps are taken to introduce Paideia reforms into our schools.

Many teachers at work in our schools are probably much better than they now have any chance of showing. Nearly all teachers sincerely wish to be good teachers and to enjoy the rewards of successful teaching. If they are freed from the onerous grind of their present occupational burdens, they can readily be inspired by the intellectual attractions of the Paideia program. They will carry many of the less competent teachers along with them, especially if, under a principal who functions as an educational leader, collaborative teaching is encouraged and arranged.

QUESTION 24: *You have differentiated three modes of teaching: didactic teaching for subject-matter instruction, coaching for intellectual skills, and Socratic or maieutic teaching for the conduct of seminar discussions.*

Does this imply that a Paideia school will have three distinct types of teachers on its instructional staff? If not, do you envisage every member of the staff as being competent in all three modes of teaching and as teaching in all three ways?

ANSWER: It is an indisputable fact that teachers are now trained chiefly in the didactic mode of teaching. Few are trained for coaching, and almost none for Socratic questioning. Current practices in teacher-training have short-changed teachers educationally. Training teachers to be good lecturers is, in fact, more difficult than training them to coach and to conduct discussions.

Since a relatively small number have received training as coaches, and few, if any at all, have been trained for Socratic teaching and the conduct of seminars, it would be unreasonable to expect all members of a school's instructional staff to engage at the outset in all three modes of teaching.

Yet among them some will have natural gifts that dispose them to take on the coaching skills or the conducting of discussions. They should, at the outset, be given the time and the opportunity to try their hand at those modes of teaching, with whatever help and guidance can be afforded them by supervision.

Ideally, as progress is made toward the full realization of the Paideia proposal, every teacher should be competent and comfortable in all three modes of teaching. Some division of labor may still be retained in the distribution of instructional tasks, but, even so, the intellectual vitality of teachers will be heightened if they are given the chance to shift from one type of teaching to another; even more so, by their being able to perform concurrently in all three ways.

QUESTION 25: *Does* The Paideia Proposal *require teachers to be competent in all areas of the subjects to be taught didactically? Or, if not all subjects, then at least more than one—the one in which that teacher majored in college or in the course of teacher training?*

ANSWER: The Paideia proposal aims to produce generalists, not specialists, in the student body. The more the members of the teaching staff are themselves generalists rather than specialists, the more effectively this objective will be achieved.

Right now at the elementary levels of instruction, teachers are expected to be generalists, though even at this level there are specialist teachers for certain skills. It is later in the departmentalized structure of the intermediate and high school that specialization becomes the rule rather than the exception.

If we still insist upon the ideal of the generalist teacher as the best instrument of instruction in a program that is generalist in aim and content, we do so with the hope that good teachers are good precisely because they have an aptitude and appetite for learning. Consequently, it is not a vain hope that, as Paideia schools develop, their teachers will also develop by degrees into being generalists, acquiring competence for the didactic teaching of additional subjects.

In this connection, please note that, although didactic instruction in mathematics occurs in Column One and the coaching of mathematical skills occurs in Column Two, the same teacher should instruct students in both aspects of mathematics. Mathematics is a body of knowledge to be didactically taught and systematically learned; it is at the same time a set of operational skills, consisting of habits developed by coaching.

The same connection holds for knowledge about language in Column One and the development of all the linguistic skills in Column Two. The study of literature and of the other arts appears in Column One, but these same subjects also appear in Column Three, where important books and other artistic productions constitute the materials for seminar discussions conducted Socratically.

When we call for the interaction and integration of the three kinds of learning and teaching, we are in effect recommending that teachers engage in all three kinds of instruction in so far as a given subject, such as mathematics, language, literature, science, or history, presents a different aspect in two or all three of the columns.

QUESTION 26: *Does not coaching, especially with regard to the skill of writing, require, on the part of students, that they do much more than is now expected of them and also, on the part of teachers, that they spend much more time in criticizing and commenting on the written work turned in?*

ANSWER: To both parts of the question, the answer is emphatically yes. Time must be allowed for this during school hours as well as after school. No satisfactory short-cut is possible here.

What is true of writing holds for other skills, though, perhaps, to a lesser degree. Time must be provided for coaching students how to read interpretatively and critically and for sessions in which students attempt to give explications of difficult texts, are criticized for their deficiencies, and are shown ways of doing better. Speaking, of course, is another skill that can be acquired only by frequent exercise under supervision.

(5) *Questions About Matters of Organization, Administration, and Financing*

QUESTION 27: *Does the size of a school make a difference to the possibility of success in carrying out the Paideia program?*

ANSWER: As long as teachers and students can gather in numbers appropriate to the mode of teaching and learning that is to be carried on, the overall size of the school should have no effect on the success of the venture.

QUESTION 28: *Ideally, what should the appropriate numbers be—what should the teacher-student ratios be—for the different modes of teaching?*

ANSWER: Unless the word "ideally" is stressed in answering this question, it cannot be answered here. It must be left to actual practitioners involved in carrying out the Paideia plan. They will reach different decisions, controlled by the different circumstances under which they find themselves operating.

Didactic teaching can be done well in a class of thirty-five or forty. It can also be done in a large lecture hall or laboratory theatre with a much larger attendance—as large as the acoustical and optical facilities can comfortably accommodate. This also holds for the use of closed-circuit television to present lectures by teachers not on the school's staff.

The coaching of intellectual skills cannot be done well with a ratio of more than ten to one; it will be better done when the ratio is larger—nearer five or six to one.

Socratic teaching in the seminar fashion should have at least fifteen students and can have as many as twenty, at most twenty-five, and it can be rendered more lively by having two seminar leaders instead of one.

QUESTION 29: *Will the Paideia program require structural changes in school buildings? Should there be different types of rooms for different modes of teaching and learning?*

ANSWER: Again, circumstances will determine the answer. The ordinary classroom—and the exceptional lecture hall or laboratory theatre—is suitable for didactic teaching. It was designed for that purpose and suits little else. But already in many schools the "open classroom" offers the opportunity to carry on coaching and seminar discussions in appropriate and congenial surroundings.

The image of a gymnasium, or of an art studio, should be kept in mind in thinking about the kind of room best adapted to coaching intellectual skills. The coach should be able to move around and amidst the small group of students whose performance he is supervising—directing and correcting. The students should all be working in his immediate vicinity and under his watchful eye and within the reach of his hand.

61

As for Socratic teaching in the seminar fashion, what is needed is a room ample enough in area to permit the introduction of a hollow square table, around which all participants, both students and teachers, sit, able to see one another and talk to one another in the cross-fire of a lively conversation. A classroom with fixed seats, set in rows, simply will not do for this purpose.

QUESTION 30: *Does the Paideia program call for a daily and weekly schedule of class hours different from the customary schedules now in operation?*

ANSWER: Yes, it does, and once again attention must be called to the difference between a blueprint answer to the question and the various answers to it that can be given by those on the spot.

In general, the self-contained elementary school classroom, with one teacher teaching the same students throughout the day, has sufficient flexibility to accommodate the different amounts of time best suited for didactic teaching, for coaching, and for seminar discussions.

At the middle or high school levels, where the customary schedule is divided into a number of 45–55 minute periods, with 5–7 minutes for moving from one class to another, changes will have to be made to accommodate the time spans needed for coaching and for seminars. The 45–55 minute period will not do for either.

Let it be said once more that the foregoing is no more than suggestive. Scheduling problems can be solved in different ways. The actual solution must be left to practitioners in the field, as the following chapter will confirm.

QUESTION 31: *Will the Paideia program in full operation cost more than the existing programs?*

ANSWER: Until Paideia schools come into existence and experience is acquired in their operation, it is impossible to answer this question with any degree of assurance. Comparative cost accounting can only be done with actual details in hand.

However, there are grounds for estimating that predictable costs are likely to be at the same level as now or even at a lower level. The reason for thinking so is the removal of costs incurred in many parts of the present school program that the Paideia proposal eliminates entirely. The savings thus made are likely to exceed the cost of the Paideia innovations.

Be that as it may, the question to be most seriously faced is not the financial one of whether as a society we can afford whatever the Paideia program costs to install and operate. Rather it is the large social, political, and human question of whether we can afford not to do it, whatever the price.

The changing state of technology and of international competition in business make the Paideia program imperative regardless of cost. As the manufacturing tasks that vocational training was once thought to prepare young Americans for are being progressively exported to other countries or eliminated by high technology, general, liberal schooling for all becomes a necessity, not a luxury.

Soon, most jobs will be *thinking* jobs requiring higher levels of reasoning, computing, analytical skills, and decision-making techniques. In the emerging economy, unlike that of the past, workers will be paid to think, to adopt techniques, to solve problems, to make decisions, and not simply to perform manual operations that machines can do better and faster.

America's competitive advantage lies in its achievements in science, in technology, and in the so-called knowledge and information industries. If this nation fails to fully develop its human resources accordingly, its competitive position in the world will precipitously decline.

5
Problems of Implementation

THE MEMBERS of the Paideia Group are thoroughly aware that they are projecting an ideal plan. They have no illusions about the distance that lies between that plan as formulated and its realization in practice. Nor do they lack appreciation of the difficulties to be encountered in the process, or the length of time it will take to make substantial progress toward the beckoning goals.

Only by the gradual accumulation of many small steps, each in the right direction, will the substantial and significant changes that we hope for make the difference in the nation's educational system that will be acknowledged as a revolution that has succeeded—succeeded as much as any revolution can succeed that seeks for a radical change in one of the basic institutions of society.

So far we have answered only those questions that ask for clarification of the theory we have proposed. Even there, some of our answers are problematic rather than definitive. What remains to be considered are the truly practical problems on the level of action—problems of implementation.

We hasten to admit that we do not know the solutions, definitely or with full assurance; first, because workable solutions will turn out to be many and various; second, because effective

65

practical thinking about problems of implementation can be done only by those who are in a position to deal with them—those on the firing line.

There is no one right answer to questions about how to do what needs to be done. Nor can one come up with any of the possible right answers except in the light of the concrete circumstances to be taken into account.

What we can offer here are suggestions for the handling of such problems. We cannot speak about all or most of them. Implementation is always concrete and particular—the here and now, the how and the who come together to determine what happens as it occurs.

With regard to some of the problems of implementation that have been brought to our attention, we offer some tentative general suggestions on the pages that follow. In addition, three members of the Paideia Group—Ruth Love (General Superintendent of Schools in the City of Chicago), Alonzo Crim (Superintendent of Schools in Atlanta, Georgia), and Nicholas Caputi (Principal of Skyline High School in Oakland, California)—have contributed accounts of what they have done or are planning to do about implementing the Paideia proposal in schools under their jurisdiction.

These statements are presented in Appendix II. They range from controlling insights about what is involved in implementing the plan to quite concrete suggestions of particular steps to be taken, specific arrangements to be set up, and innovative devices to be employed.

As was to be expected—it is in fact reassuring—some overlap will be found in the contents of these three statements. But they are also sufficiently diverse in approach to deserve close attention. In any case, they come from competent educational practitioners who are in day to day contact with the problems and practices of our schools, and who are fully cognizant of all the realities—all the difficulties—that confront anyone who undertakes to change basic schooling in the direction proposed.

PROBLEM 1: *How should courses be organized in a Paideia School? Should the diagram that depicts the framework for a Paideia curriculum be interpreted as calling for three different kinds of courses that correspond to the three kinds of learning and teaching? Didactic instruction to help students acquire knowledge of the basic fields of subject-matters appears to suggest another set of courses, one for each of the subject-matters named in Column One of the diagram. How does this all fit together?*

SUGGESTION: In the first place, what is said in the footnote to the diagram must be repeated here: "The three columns do not correspond to separate courses, nor is one kind of teaching and learning necessarily confined to any one class."

In the second place, the subject-matters named in Column One represent subject-matters that have been didactically taught in our schools for many years. We have courses in mathematics; courses in biology, chemistry, and physics; courses in history, in geography, 'and in the study of social institutions; courses in the study of foreign languages; courses in literature and the other arts, such as music and the visual arts.

The retention of such subject-matter courses in the Paideia curriculum introduces nothing novel. The only suggested innovation is that the Paideia curriculum should start didactic instruction in all these subjects in the elementary grades and continue to advanced levels of difficulty at the intermediate and secondary grades. More important and also more innovative is the suggestion that coaching in all the intellectual skills—both in the language arts and in the techniques of mathematical operations and of scientific procedures—should be intimately related to didactic instruction in the subjects listed in Column One.

Lastly, the books to be read and discussed in seminars, as well as other works of art experienced and discussed, should correspond to the range of subject-matter covered by didactic instruction.

How the coaching of skills and the Socratic discussion of basic ideas and values are to be integrated with didactic instruction in areas of subject-matter will vary as students pass from the elementary through the intermediate to the secondary grades of basic schooling. At each level, there are many different ways in which this can be done. The choice of one or another must be left to the practitioners.

But we must sound a warning. Because it is the mode of teaching and learning that now almost exclusively occupies school time, and because this has been true for many decades, didactic teaching may threaten to dominate the program, to the subordination and the detriment of the other two modes of teaching. This must not be allowed to happen in any school that is conscientiously dedicated to constructing a Paideia course of study for all twelve years and for all students.

PROBLEM 2: *How should the Paideia plan be implemented in a school system? Should it be tried in a model school that puts the plan into operation for all twelve grades? Or in a whole school system?*

Might it not be more feasible to start in the upper grades, either the last four years or the last six, instead of all twelve at once?

Would it not be prudent to begin with a partial implementation of the plan, partial either with respect to the grades involved, or partial with respect to the kind of teaching and learning involved, rather than attempt a total implementation from the very beginning?

SUGGESTION: These questions by no means exhaust the several and various ways in which a school system can implement the Paideia plan. There is no way of deciding which of these ways is best, or whether some other way is still better. But something can be said that bears on these alternatives.

Any scheme of implementation, no matter how or where it begins, should aim ultimately at having the Paideia program in operation for *all* twelve years and for *all* three kinds of learning and teaching. Nothing less than this would be a thorough-going test and an adequate approach to the attainment of the desired objectives.

We are not willing to settle for a "Paideia high school" because, in our judgment, no reform of secondary schooling is likely to succeed if it is not built upon a successful reform of the first eight grades.

Nor are we willing to settle for the introduction of some coaching in certain skills rather than all; or for the introduction of a smattering of seminar discussions here and there, rather than a thorough effort to see that Socratic teaching occurs in all grades.

This does not mean that we are against partial implementations of one sort or another *at the beginning*. In fact, in Chap-

69

ter Six, we shall have some suggestions to offer about different ways to begin.

PROBLEM 3:   *In the implementation of the Paideia program, it will be necessary to select certain materials (e.g., textbooks, workbooks, etc.) to be used in the didactic teaching of the basic subjects. It will be necessary to employ certain methods as well as materials in the coaching of the intellectual skills. It will be necessary to draw up a list of books to be read through twelve years of seminars, as well as a list of works of art to be studied and discussed.*

The Paideia Proposal *is, for the most part, silent about all these important prerequisites. Without them, implementation cannot get very far. Can the Paideia Group give us any help in the solution of this problem?*

SUGGESTION: We were silent about these prerequisites in *The Paideia Proposal* because it would take a whole book to deal with them. But as we announced in the Proposal, and here as well, that book will be written in the form of a collection of essays by members of the Paideia Group. It will set forth suggestions about the materials, methods, and measures to be employed in the teaching of every element in a course of study constructed within the curricular framework proposed.

The essays will naturally be only suggestive, only indications of what can be done. They will not provide the one and only definitive answer to the question.

PROBLEM 4:   *It would seem that the study of Latin or Greek is more consonant with the tenor of the Paideia plan than the study of one or another modern language—certainly for the sake of understanding language itself, even if not for reasons*

70

of practical utility. Is the Paideia Group in favor of or opposed to the substitution of Latin or Greek for a modern European or Asiatic language?

COMMENT: We are neither for nor against the substitution of Latin or Greek as options within the requirement of a second language. The decision rests entirely with the school authorities.

PROBLEM 5: *How many years should be devoted to each element in the Paideia curriculum—for the study of a second language, of mathematics and the natural sciences, of history, geography, and social institutions? How many years should be devoted to the coaching of intellectual skills and to Socratically conducted seminars? How many for physical education, for manual training, and for a general introduction to the world of work?*

COMMENT: Some of these questions have already been definitively answered in *The Paideia Proposal:* twelve years for the coaching of intellectual skills; twelve years for the Socratically conducted seminars; twelve years for physical education.

For all the rest, we have suggested the last year or two of the twelve for a general introduction to the world of work; about six years for manual training and related crafts. These are very tentative suggestions. Beyond this we must remain silent and leave decisions about time allotments to the local curriculum makers.

PROBLEM 6: *You have recommended pre-school tutoring for children in need of such help to prepare them to enter school on a more nearly equal basis with others who come from more favorable home environments. You have also recommended*

71

supplementary instruction to help students who are lagging behind their fellows in this or that phase of the curriculum.

Both of these things will have to be done at the public expense. Have you any suggestion about how their cost will be underwritten, how children will be selected for pre-school study or for supplemental instruction, how much time will be devoted to these activities, and how teachers will be used in this part of the plan.

COMMENT: In our judgment, all of these matters must be left to state legislatures, state commissioners of education, and to local school districts and their heads or superintendents.

PROBLEM 7:   *You are obviously concerned with the training and competence of the teaching staffs that will be engaged in implementing the Paideia plan. Would you recommend some scheme for the certification of teachers?*

COMMENT: Many thorny difficulties confront us in this matter of certifying teachers. Recent criticisms of the bar examinations for the legal profession and the medical board examinations for the certification of physicians have called attention to some of them. We therefore hesitate to recommend or to reject any scheme for the certification of teachers. But we strongly believe that places should be found for persons who show themselves to be good teachers even if they are not certified.

The problem of teacher competency is more fruitfully approached by making whatever changes are necessary in the *training* of future teachers. Something must emerge that is radically different from the present ways in which teachers are trained in existing schools or departments of education.

72

In Chapter 8 of *The Paideia Proposal* we ventured some suggestions about the shape such training should take. We are contemplating the establishment of a Paideia Center, which would function in a consultative fashion and would take on as one of its tasks this matter of teacher training. It might even eventually develop into a Paideia school of education.

As for the question of professional standards, the answer is the same for the teaching profession as it is for any other—law, medicine, engineering, accountancy, the military, and so on. To perform the services that a particular profession is intent upon offering, a person should be dedicated to its ideal goal— the human and social goods that are needed and that require both expert knowledge and skill, and also ethical performance. It is that dedication which distinguishes the professional person from those engaged in work solely for the sake of making money.

This is not to say that professionals should not be adequately compensated for the work they do. But those who teach only because that is a convenient way of earning a living, who would rather not teach if they could earn a living some other way, and who would not teach at all if they did not have to earn a living, lack the motivation that characterizes a truly professional person.

6
A Pair of Entering Wedges

LEAVING THE STEPS of implementation to practitioners on the spot, we go on to some general recommendations about the ways in which a school or school system can begin to implement the Paideia program.

Our first suggestion for an entering wedge—an initial and obviously partial effort to implement the program—comes from our awareness of what is almost completely absent from existing courses of study at all levels of basic schooling, except perhaps the kindergarten and the first few grades. In very few public schools, at any level above kindergarten and the first few grades, can we find courses in which students discuss books as well as other works of art. What is absent, in short, is the most important of the three kinds of learning and of teaching—the kind that results in an expanded and deepened understanding of basic ideas and values.

This deplorable deficiency should certainly be remedied first. Here, then, is one entering wedge in implementing the Paideia program. Socratically conducted discussions, based on the reading of books that are not textbooks, or on the experience of music, dance, or the graphic arts should be instituted as the most desirable initial improvement of the present curriculum. Wherever feasible, this first effort should be undertaken in all twelve years—not confined to the upper grades.

It will, of course, be easier to set up such seminars for students in high school, easiest of all for juniors and seniors there. But the entering wedge would exert much greater force, opening the gate to further Paideia reforms, if Socratic teaching were introduced in the third, fourth, and fifth grades, and on up.

A second entering wedge of nearly equal importance would be to improve and strengthen such coaching of intellectual skills as now exists and then extend this kind of teaching and learning to skills that are now either very poorly developed, or not developed at all; for example, skill in reading beyond the elementary level, skill in speaking, and skill in listening, with their parallel skills in performing mathematical operations and scientific procedures.

Here again, the effort should be made across the board—for all the requisite skills and for all twelve grades. Further, the introduction of this second entering wedge will be more effective in proportion as it is more and more integrated with the seminars. That integration can be achieved by having writing done that draws upon what has been learned in the seminars, by having students give talks or make speeches about the same subjects on which they have written, by checking on how well they have listened to the discussions, and by ascertaining how well they have read the books discussed.

With these two entering wedges working in concert, the reform of the course of study can move to the first column in the diagram and spur efforts to improve didactic teaching in all the basic subject-matters.

Improvement there will result, first, from a better conception of what should be learned with respect to each of these subject-matters; second, from an effort to integrate the third kind of teaching and learning with the other two; and third, most important of all, from observing the maxim that "less is more," thus curtailing the effort to be comprehensive in covering subject-matter, substituting for it the effort to be sure that whatever ground is covered has been thoroughly digested and assimilated.*

* One member of the Paideia Group, Theodore Sizer, with extensive and widely varied experience in dealing with public and private schools all over the country, has other suggestions to make concerning how a school or school system should begin in its efforts to implement the Paideia principles. These suggestions are set forth in Appendix III.

7
The Possibilities

To TAKE ADVANTAGE of possibilities, we must believe that they exist. Disbelief arises from a confusion of the difficult with the impossible. Many things are difficult; few, if any—even the most vexatiously difficult—are impossible. The most frequent mistake we are apt to make is to convert the merely improbable into the impossible, where the degree of improbability rises high because of the many and serious difficulties that stand in the way of turning what is genuinely possible into an actual reality.

As the preceding chapters have shown, there are many and serious difficulties to be overcome, many problems to be solved, in order to actualize the Paideia plan in some satisfactory, approximate form. Recognizing the difficulty of a problem should not lead us to turn our back on it as insoluble. Confronting difficulties, however troublesome, should not cause us to despair and try to by-pass them as if they were insurmountable.

In practical matters, one other mistake we too often make is more destructive than any other. It is the mistake of abandoning the general principles that serve to direct and guide our actions because there are difficulties to overcome and concrete problems to be solved in applying those general principles to the particular circumstances in which we find ourselves. We mistakenly yield to the temptation to follow the line of other principles even though that line is alien to our original purpose.

One other thing may derail the implementation of a theoretically formulated plan. Those who are burdened with making decisions from day to day too often dismiss theory as too remote from the hurly-burly of action to be taken seriously. Even worse, they are ready to discard theory and principles as impracticable, because they are stumped as to how to act in the pursuit of what they initially accepted as sound.

In Chapter One of this book, we referred to those who take issue with the Paideia principles by raising objections to the ends appointed or challenging the general means recommended for achieving them. We have not answered such objections or challenges. A substantial majority of the comments we have received—in reviews, conferences, and public discussions of *The Paideia Proposal*—do not regard the reform proposed as being aimed in the wrong direction and do not reject the recommendation of the means as not the right prescription for achieving the appointed goals.* Our discussion in these pages has therefore been an attempt to answer the questions raised by those who approve the Paideia principles. We have suggested solutions to the problems of implementing them.

If we have heard any undercurrent of dissent or doubt from those who endorse the Paideia principles, it has been about the feasibility under present-day circumstances of implementing the plan. These doubts, if unallayed, may lead practitioners to think that the ideals that guide our reform are utopian—not merely difficult to realize, but impossible.

---

*See Appendix I for an inventory of these reviews, conferences, and discussions, in which both favorable comments and adverse criticisms have occurred.

Giving all the children of this country the same high quality of basic schooling is certainly not unthinkable. It is not a self-evident impossibility, and so the dismissal of it as utopian must itself be dismissed as groundless.

Everyone is willing to agree that at least some portion of our school population can be given the high quality of basic schooling that we recommend. It is only when the recommendation is extended from *some* to *all* that anyone becomes skeptical and demurs on the grounds that we are going beyond the bounds of the possible. They are then inclined to turn aside and busy themselves with things much easier for them to do. But these easier things leave unsolved the problem of giving all the children equal educational opportunity. It is these easier things that are really impractical for the stated feasible purpose that we cannot—we dare not—abandon.

To sum up: the Paideia plan is not utopian. There is no empirical evidence that its recommendations go beyond the bounds of the possible. What it calls for has never been tried. We cannot say, as if we knew from actual experience, that schools are being asked to do what cannot be done.

In the second place, the directive principles of the Paideia plan should not be deemed unworkable because certain difficulties stand in the way of its implementation. If they are the right principles, to abandon them leads either to the substitution of unsound principles for them (because easier to apply) or to proceeding without any guiding principles at all (because then no problems of application remain).

Finally, in a difficult situation, it is a mistake to give up too soon. One attempt at application may fail, and still another, but that does not call for total surrender. We should not set any limits to our ingenuity at innovation. If our directive principles are sound, we have no choice but to persevere in the effort to find the particular, concrete means needed to apply them effectively.

We think it is now sufficiently clear that *The Paideia Proposal* has persuaded a large number of administrators, teachers, school boards, and others concerned with basic schooling in this country—persuaded them of the rightness of the goals and of the soundness and indispensability of the general means recommended. We believe that such persuaded practitioners will eventually achieve a substantial measure of success if they do not despair because of all the obstacles to be surmounted and all the difficult problems to be solved.

They must persist in the knowledge that whatever is within the bounds of possibility can be done. They must proceed with faith in their own ingenuity to cut through Gordian knots. They must have the courage to stumble through hours of darkness to the dawn of a new day for our public schools.

Appendix I

Section A

A list of reviews, articles, and critical notices in magazines and newspapers, unfavorable as well as favorable.

Education USA (National School Public Relations Association), Vol. 24, No. 25, February 15, 1982

Boston Sunday Globe, February 21 and May 23, 1982

The Dallas Morning News, February 22, 1982

The Christian Science Monitor, June 28, 1982

The American School Board Journal (National School Boards Association), Vol. 169, No. 7, July 1982

The Denver Post, August 26, 1982

The New York Times, August 17 and 22, 1982

Chicago Sun-Times, August 22, 1982

Fort Worth Star-Telegram, August 22, 1982

Education Times, August 30, 1982

Journal (American Library Association), August 1982

Booklist (American Library Association), September 1, 1982

The Oregonian (Portland), September 5, 1982

Time, September 6, 1982

Chicago Tribune, September 12, 1982

Los Angeles Times, September 12, 1982

Appendix I

The Detroit News, September 13, 1982

The Torch (St. John's University, Jamaica, New York), September 15, 1982

The Kansas City Times, September 17 and 22, 1982

Michigan Chronicle (Detroit), September 18, 1982

America, September 18, 1982

The Denver Post, September 26, 1982

The Sun (Baltimore), September 26, 1982

Virginia-Pilot Ledger Star (Norfolk), September 26, 1982

The Rotarian (Rotary International), Vol. 141, No. 3, September 1982

The Washington Monthly, September 1982

The Stockton Record (California), October 3, 1982

The Boston Globe, October 11, 1982

Basic Education (Council for Basic Education), Vol. 27, No. 2, October 1982

Education Week, November 3 and 24, 1982

The Center Magazine (The Robert Maynard Hutchins Center for the Study of Democratic Institutions), Santa Barbara, California, November/December 1982

San Francisco Examiner, December 1982

American Educator (American Federation of Teachers), Vol. 6, No. 4, Winter 1982

Pioneer Press & Dispatch (St. Paul, Minnesota), January 1, 1983

Kliatt Young Adult Paperback Book Guide, January 1983

Commentary, January 1983

Grand Forks Herald (North Dakota), February 24, 1983

84

The Atlanta Journal-Constitution, March 6, 1983

The Arizona Republic (Phoenix), March 10, 1983

The Peninsula Times Tribune (California), March 14, 1983

ASCD Update (Association for Supervision and Curriculum Development), Vol. 25, No. 2, March 1983

Harvard Educational Review, Vol. 53, No. 4, October 1983

Section B

A list of educational conferences and meetings.

PRIOR TO THE PUBLICATION OF *The Paideia Proposal*

Special Conference of the Fifty State Commissioners of Education, Washington, D.C.

Charles Wright Academy, Tacoma, Washington

Basic Skills National Technical Assistance Consortium, St. Louis, Missouri

Council of the Great City Schools, Memphis, Tennessee

National Institute of Education, U.S. Department of Education, Washington, D.C.

The Association for Supervision and Curriculum Development, Alexandria, Virginia

Meeting of New England Educators at Harvard University, Cambridge, Massachusetts

National School Boards Association, Washington, D.C.

The National Association of Secondary School Principals, Reston, Virginia

North Shore Country Day School, Wilmette, Illinois

Urban Superintendents' Network, Washington, D.C.

Appendix I

Special Luncheon for seventy-five educators in Texas

Special Luncheon for educators and citizens of Minneapolis-St. Paul at the University of Minnesota

Meetings with educators in North Carolina at the University of North Carolina

Conference of educators at the Graduate School of Education at the University of Southern California, Los Angeles

Meeting with educators and citizens at the University of San Francisco

Conference of educators and members of government in Washington, D.C.

Meeting with the Maryland Superintendents of Schools

Conference with members of the Educational Leadership Forum

Conference at the School of Education at the University of Chicago

National Institute of Education, Washington, D.C.

Bank Street College of Education, New York City

Mississippi Association of Colleges, Jackson

Johnson Foundation Conference on Studies of High Schools, Wisconsin

U.S. Department of Education, Region V, Mid-Western States

College Board's National Forum, Washington, D.C.

Illinois State Board of Education, Springfield

Superintendents of Schools, Department of Education, San Diego County, California

86

Anaheim Conference, Department of Education, San Diego County, California

Retired Schoolmaster's Council (Rossmoor), Walnut Creek, California

Principals of the Oakland Unified School District, California

Norwalk Board of Cooperative Educational Services, Connecticut

Colorado Academy, Denver

University of North Dakota, Grand Forks

American Association of School Administrators, Arlington, Virginia

Springfield City Schools, Ohio

Arizona Humanities Council, Phoenix

York University, Downsview, Ontario, Canada

National University Continuing Education Association, Washington, D.C.

American Federation of Teachers, Washington, D.C.

Mount Saint Mary's College, Emmitsburg, Maryland

William Rainey Harper College, Palatine, Illinois

Universidad Interamericana de Puerto Rico, Hato Rey

The Grosse Pointe Public School System, Michigan

St. John's College, Santa Fe, New Mexico

The Robert Maynard Hutchins Center for the Study of Democratic Institutions, Santa Barbara, California

New Hampshire Association for Supervision and Curriculum Department, Nashua

Wyoming, Ohio, Board of Education

Ontario Council of Teachers of English, Downsview, Ontario, Canada

Appendix I

Moravian College, Bethlehem, Pennsylvania

American Educational Studies Association, Milwaukee, Wisconsin

Arkansas College, Batesville

Superintendents, Trustees, and Principals of Contra Costa, San Joaquin, Stanislaus, and Tuolumne Counties, California

University of Nebraska, Lincoln

National Council of Teachers of English, Urbana, Illinois

Southern Association of Colleges and Schools, Atlanta, Georgia

Aspen Institute of Humanistic Studies, Board of Directors

The Wisconsin Association of Teacher Educators, University of Wisconsin, Madison

Independent School Association of the Central States, Downers Grove, Illinois

California Coalition for Fair School Finance (League of Women Voters of California, California State PTA, American Association of University Women)

Grand Rapids Area Council for the Humanities, Michigan

Fortnightly Club, Dallas, Texas

American Association of Higher Education, Washington, D.C.

Kentucky State University and the Frankfort Arts Foundation

Connecticut Educational Services, New Haven

University of Northern Colorado, Greeley

The Cambridge School of Weston, Massachusetts

Northfield Mount Hermon, Massachusetts

The Putney School, Vermont

Section C

A list of interviews on television and radio.

KIRO-Radio, Seattle, Washington

Paideia Demonstration Seminar, WNET-TV, New York

WEBR-Radio, Buffalo, New York

KVI-Radio, Seattle, Washington

Two-hour interview on "Extension 720," with Milt Rosenberg, WGN-Radio, Chicago

Taping interview for Nashville, Tennessee, Evening News, WTVF-TV

Mortimer Adler and Alonzo Crim, appearance on "Good Morning, America" with David Hartmann, ABC-TV, New York

WABC-Radio, New York

Interview on "The Sherrye Henry Show," WOR-Radio, New York

Appearance on "Daybreak," with Judy Moen, WBBM-TV, Chicago

Interview on "The David Baum Show," WIND-Radio, Chicago

KTOK-Radio, Oklahoma City

WHO-Radio, Des Moines, Iowa

Interview on "Open Forum," syndicated by Public Interest Affiliates, with Hope Daniels, WLOO, WAIT-Radio, Chicago

Interview on "The Owen Spann Show," KGO-Radio, San Francisco

Interview on "Today in Chicago," with Jorie Lueloff, WMAQ-TV, Chicago

Mortimer Adler and Ruth Love, interview on "Live at Lawry's," with Sondra Gair, WBEZ-Radio, Chicago

Appendix I

Appearance on "Cromie's Circle," with Bob Cromie, WGN-TV, Chicago

Appearance on "Firing Line," with William F. Buckley, Jr., WNET-TV, New York

WGST-Radio, Atlanta, Georgia

WHA-Radio, Madison, Wisconsin

Interview on "Take Two," with Don Farmer and Chris Curle, CNN (Cable News Network), Atlanta, Georgia

Appendix II

Section A

Statement by Ruth Love, General Superintendent of Schools in the City of Chicago.

In the Chicago school system, our planning for the implementation of *The Paideia Proposal* has been initially concerned with the following four problems: (1) the problem of different possible patterns of implementation; (2) the problem of course organization; (3) the problem of teacher retraining; and (4) the problem of school organization and scheduling.

(1)

Patterns of Implementation

Educators adopt the Paideia plan for an *entire* school system only after its being tested and validated. The best vehicle for testing the Paideia plan is to implement it on a pilot basis. This may mean one or several Paideia schools initially. Since the Paideia plan is a program for the twelve years of compulsory schooling, the following patterns of implementation deserve consideration.

(a) *Immersion Pattern* (grades 1–6): In a separate school, utilizing an existing or new structure. The number of years to complete the pilot cycle (enroll and graduate students from grade 12) would be five. (See Attachment A for a sample illustration.)

(b) *Immersion Pattern* (grades 1–8): In a separate school, utilizing an existing or new structure. Here the number of years to complete the pilot cycle would be seven. (See Attachment B for a sample illustration.)

(c) *Gradual Phase-in Plan* (initially grades 1, 5, and 9): A school-within-a-school design, utilizing an existing elementary and high school in a *centrally located district* to promote access to the program from all geographic areas of the city. In this gradual phase-in plan, Paideia students would be enrolled into grades 1, 5, and 9 during the first pilot year. After four years, the first generation Paideia students would have progressed to grades 5, 9, and 12, respectively. (See Attachment C for a sample illustration.)

At the very least, a school system might initiate activities and programs that would engage students in Column Three learning activities, the most neglected form of learning and mode of teaching in our present educational offerings. Initiating Socratically conducted seminars in which students at all levels probe the answers to "why" questions, discuss books and works of art, and thereby expand and deepen their understanding of ideas and values, might take several forms, such as:

- utilizing study hall periods for supervised reading and Socratically conducted discussion of selected books, essays, poems, etc.

- extending the school day twice weekly to accommodate supervised reading and Socratically conducted discussion of selected books, essays, poems, etc.

- revising English, social studies, and science curricula to include the reading of selected works and their discussion in the Socratic manner.

- engaging selected staff in a training program to teach them to conduct discussions in the Socratic manner (*e.g.* through after-school training programs or through Teacher Institutes held during the summer and/or on Saturdays).

(2)

Course Organization

Ideally, courses should *integrate* the three modes of instruction. This is easier to achieve in the lower grades, where classrooms are self-contained; in the middle and upper grades, students might receive didactic instruction in subjects such as geography, mathematics, science, and literature three days a week. The two remaining days would be devoted to coaching students in the development of skills and seminar discussions.

For example, Monday, Wednesday, and Friday could be devoted to didactic instruction (lecture and demonstration); Tuesday and Thursday could be devoted to coaching sessions in the various skill areas and to seminars.

Further, adoption of the Paideia program would require that more time be spent in the lower grades than is currently spent on subjects such as science, social studies, and geography.

(3)

Teacher Retraining

Initially, the focus here must be upon *retraining* the current teaching staff to carry out the Paideia program. This includes: strengthening knowledge of subjects; developing coaching skills; and developing the skills needed to conduct seminars using the Socratic method.

In order to achieve these staff development goals, an ongoing teacher retraining program is essential. Initially, this would involve teacher institutes in conjunction with universities (summer and/or Saturday institutes); training would consist of reading and discussing selected works, participating in and observing a model Socratically conducted seminar, conducting a seminar oneself, and being observed and coached by an expert.

Additionally, teachers who participate in extensive teacher retraining institutes should receive a certificate of accomplishment; later a Paideia endorsement on existing certificates would be required for appointment to a Paideia school.

(4)

School Organization and Scheduling

How can the school day be structured, students scheduled, and staff deployed to accommodate effective teaching and learning in all three columns?

This problem can be addressed in numerous ways. What is essential is to recognize that scheduling patterns *different from* the traditional ten forty-minute daily class periods will be necessary to carry out effectively the Paideia program.

Specifically, didactic instruction in fundamental subjects (Column One) can be done effectively in groups of thirty to fifty students gathered in a lecture hall or auditorium.

Coaching students in the development of intellectual skills (Column Two) can be done effectively in a traditional classroom by clustering desks into specific skill development groups made up of five or six students.

The coach-student cluster ratio should not exceed 6:1. The coach may move from one cluster to another supervising practice. College students and accelerated Paideia students can be trained as coaches.

Seminar discussion in the Socratic mode should take place in groups of twenty to twenty-five students seated around a hollow square table.

Students should be grouped by achievement/ability for coaching sessions. Students who manifest persistent deficiencies must spend

A Sample Paideia Student Schedule

Monday	Tuesday	Wednesday	Thursday	Friday
Lecture/ Demo	Coaching in Mathematics (2-hour session)	Same as Monday	2-hour Seminar	Same as Monday
Lecture/ Demo				
Break	Break		Break	
Lecture/ Demo	Coaching in Science/lab techniques (2-hour session)		Coaching in Writing (2-hour session)	
Lecture/ Demo				
Lunch	Lunch		Lunch	
Lecture/ Demo	Coaching in Reading, Interpretation and Vocabulary (2-hour session)		Coaching in problem solving and critical thinking (2-hour session)	
Lecture/ Demo				
Tutorial (if needed)	Tutorial (if needed)	Tutorial (if needed)	Tutorial (if needed)	Extra-Curricular

This sample schedule is based on an 8-hour day (including a 15-minute break, a 45-minute lunch period, and a 60-minute extension to accommodate remediation/enrichment tutorials and extra-curricular activities).

more time-on-task in learning centers or in after-school or weekend tutorials. Students should be grouped by achievement/ability for *some aspects of didactic instruction,* particularly mathematics. All didactic instruction should be videotaped and a library facility should be made available where students who need to hear the lesson again may do so after school.

How much time should be devoted to each of the three forms of learning? The major portion of instruction time (approximately 60 percent) should be given to the acquisition of subject-matter knowledge. The remaining 40 percent should be given to the coaching of skills and seminar discussions.

In a self-contained classroom setting, appropriate for the lower grades, the teacher can incorporate all three modes of instruction (didactic, coaching, and seminar discussion) in a weekly instruction plan, grouping students for skill coaching at appropriate times during the week. In the middle and upper grades, where instruction is departmentalized to provide more in-depth teaching of subjects, the following scheduling pattern is one possibility. Didactic instruction in the fundamental subjects should dominate (60 percent of the instruction time; perhaps on Monday, Wednesday, and Friday); coaching in the development of intellectual skills would occupy approximately 30 percent of the time; and seminar discussion, approximately 10 percent of the time, on Tuesday and Thursday. See the diagram on page 95 as an illustration of such scheduling.

ATTACHMENT A

Type: Immersion, grades 1–8

Site: Separate school; new or existing structure

Projected Enrollment: 600/675/750/825/900

Number of Students per Grade: 75

Number of Years to Complete Pilot Cycle: 5 years

Continuation Plan: enroll 75 grade 1 students each successive year

GRADES	FIRST YEAR	SECOND YEAR	THIRD YEAR	FOURTH YEAR	1988–89
1	75	75	75	75	75
2	75	75	75	75	75
3	75	75	75	75	75
4	75	75	75	75	75
5	75	75	75	75	75
6	75	75	75	75	75
7	75	75	75	75	75
8	75	75	75	75	75
9		75	75	75	75
10			75	75	75
11				75	75
12					75
Total number of students	600	675	750	825	900

ATTACHMENT B

Type: Immersion, grades 1–6

Site: Separate school; new or existing structure

Projected Enrollment: 450/525/600/675/750/825/900

Number of Students per Grade: 75

Number of Years to Complete Pilot Cycle: 7 years

Continuation Plan: enroll 75 grade 1 students each successive year

GRADES	FIRST YEAR	SECOND YEAR	THIRD YEAR	FOURTH YEAR	FIFTH YEAR	SIXTH YEAR	1990–91
1	75	75	75	75	75	75	75
2	75	75	75	75	75	75	75
3	75	75	75	75	75	75	75
4	75	75	75	75	75	75	75
5	75	75	75	75	75	75	75
6	75	75	75	75	75	75	75
7		75	75	75	75	75	75
8			75	75	75	75	75
9				75	75	75	75
10					75	75	75
11						75	75
12							75
Total number of students	450	525	600	675	750	825	900

ATTACHMENT C

Type: Gradual phase-in

Site: School-within-a-school; existing elementary and high school in
same district

Projected Enrollment: 400/800/1,200/1,600

Number of Students per Grade: see chart below

Number of Years to Complete Pilot Cycle: 4 years

Continuation Plan: enroll additional students into grades 1, 5, and 9
for three successive years

Code: [____] — new enrollees

GRADES	FIRST YEAR	SECOND YEAR	THIRD YEAR	FOURTH YEAR
1	100	100	100	100
2		100	100	100
3			100	100
4				100
5	100	100	100	100
6		100	100	100
7			100	100
8				100
9	200	200	200	200
10		200	200	200
11			200	200
12				200
Total number of **students**	400	800	1,200	1,600

Section B

Statement by Alonzo Crim, Superintendent, Atlanta (Georgia) Public Schools

The Atlanta Public Schools have been on the move since 1974 in improving reading and mathematics test scores. Increasingly, students, staff, and community members are believing that an 80 percent poor and 90 percent black school population can achieve at national norm levels or better.

When Mortimer Adler came to Atlanta in the spring of 1982 and demonstrated that twenty-five of Atlanta's students could engage effectively in Socratic seminars, the Atlanta Board of Education and administrative staff determined that *The Paideia Proposal* should be implemented in the Atlanta Public Schools. Further, Paideia would become the springboard for reform of basic schooling in our school system.

Booker T. Washington High School, once Atlanta's only high school for blacks, was selected as the major pilot site because it was starting a magnet program for the humanities. The principal, Dr. Robert Collins, and Area III Superintendent, Dr. Elizabeth Feely, thought it was a "natural" to model the magnet along the lines of *The Paideia Proposal*.

We have learned in the Atlanta Public Schools that if we wish to perform miracles, we must teach our staff how. When we established the national norms to be obtained by 1985, we took the first step toward that goal with staff development. Again, we have started a new program with staff development. We feel we cannot allow the program to fail because of our own personal failures as a staff.

The Danforth Foundation has provided the Atlanta Public Schools with a small grant to assist the school system in bringing Dr. Adler to Atlanta from one to two days each month for the 1983 school year

100

in order to help both staff and students. Many will thus be able to be with and observe a skilled teacher using the Socratic method. Adler will teach the teachers and the trainers of teachers, as well as students, in the same manner that we expect teachers to teach students.

In addition to Adler's work with staff and students, the Atlanta Public Schools have another advantage in having the national office of the National Humanities Faculty move to Atlanta. Dr. Billye Gaines, former Washington High School teacher of Russian, is now Program Director of the National Humanities Faculty. She has persuaded her colleagues to join the Washington High School faculty in making Paideia a reality. National Humanities Faculty scholars have already begun visiting Washington High School.

The National Humanities Faculty has discussed with Washington's staff its reflections on the implementation of Paideia. It has viewed and criticized demonstration lessons by several staff members who have been assigned to the project. Most important, the National Humanities Faculty has shared its enthusiasm for making use of all three of the teaching styles described in the Paideia plan. The Faculty has engaged the staff in discussion about how and when to mix and match appropriate content to student needs, and it has stimulated staff members to renew its own excitement through scholarship and discovery.

The Board of Education, students, community members, and staff are enthusiastic about the implementation of Paideia. The Atlanta community is ready for the revolutionary concept of universal schooling for all, schooling that is the same in quality as well as quantity, and with that quality at a level that exceeds the existing current national norms.

It is our intent in Atlanta to go about the business of putting this program into action while the critics of the program go on saying how impractical it is and why it cannot be implemented.

Postscript

What follows is a statement by Elizabeth Feely, Superintendent of Area III, who has worked directly with Dr. Adler on his visits to Atlanta. She is trying to implement the Paideia program in two sets of schools, each with one secondary school that is served by feeder schools, elementary and secondary. The implementation she is striving for covers the whole range of basic schooling from K through 12.

As *The Paideia Proposal* is being initiated in Area III of the Atlanta Public Schools, we face problems basic to any radical change in teaching methodology. However, the remarkable advances in education promised by these changes provide the impetus to face and overcome obstacles.

Communication is the first step. Before any change of this magnitude can be implemented, its benefits, as well as the need, must be understood throughout the academic community. A thorough knowledge of the teaching methods proposed must be acquired by all principals and teachers, backed by the support and interest of parents and community representatives. The leadership of the principal is critical to the success of the program.

First on the required reading list is *The Paideia Proposal.* Each principal and resource teacher has been given the assignment to read and study this educational manifesto.

Circulation is made of copies of articles published about *The Paideia Proposal.* Bulletin boards in the Area III office, as well as various media, will be used to convey information. Awareness of what the proposal is has been created by informing parents and business and community groups.

Commitment on the part of many is vital. There must be commitment from the staff implementing the concept. The principal of a predominantly black, inner-city high school, and the elementary and middle feeder school principals were given an option. They were advised of the serious responsibility to be placed on them and they were allowed to choose. They accepted the commitment. The principals of an integrated high school, middle school, and feeder elementary school also made the commitment to participate.

Principals were asked to identify a cadre of teachers in each school with whom they can jointly learn and from whom peers can learn. Shared observations will be made within individual schools and between schools.

Administrators and teachers in Area III, many of whom are untrained in the Socratic mode of teaching, will participate in seminars and begin conducting seminars—K through 12. Videotapes will be shared and critiqued.

Athletic coaches and musicians will demonstrate to teachers the techniques they use in coaching. Learning by doing will be emphasized. This transfer of techniques in coaching will be used to develop proficiency in reading, writing, speaking, listening, and computing.

In the absence of art teachers in the elementary feeder schools, the Area III art resource teacher developed teaching units. Teachers are being trained so that every elementary principal and teacher can adapt these for use in every classroom in order that all students experience similar exposure in fine arts. Students from elementary schools participate in the Area III Elementary Symphony Chorus.

Assembly programs are encouraged in which students perform as well as participate as an audience.

Beginning in kindergarten, teachers will read quality-approved literature daily to children. From the time a child can read, assignments will be made from a reading list. The Junior Great Books will be included. Outside reading will continue through the twelfth grade. Homework will be assigned daily.

Stress is on the quality as well as quantity of student writing. An *Area III Anthology* will continue to be published annually. In the media center of each school a book is kept containing student writings submitted monthly.

With budgetary constraints, ways must be found to provide remedial help. Volunteers will continue to be recruited from the religious, civic, business, and retirement communities. Community resources will also be used to provide enrichment for all students.

The number of electives in the present curriculum will be decreased in order to approach the complete elimination recommended by the manifesto. Supervision will be vigilant to assure that effective teaching takes place. We know the children can learn if they are taught.

Evaluation will be continuous both formally and informally, and adjustments made accordingly. Input from parents, teachers, students, administrators, and community representatives will be sought.

Sufficient time will be taken to implement *The Paideia Proposal* soundly.

Activities will be designed to put joy into learning for students as well as for principals and teachers as a result of disciplined study. As we are taught, so will we teach and so will our children learn.

Section C

Statement by Nicholas Caputi, Principal of Skyline High School in Oakland, California

Skyline High School is an urban, comprehensive school with a combined staff of 97 teachers and 40 classified employees.

The student population of over 2,000 is approximately 40 percent black, 46 percent white and 14 percent Asian, with small representation from other minorities. J. David Bowick is Superintendent of Schools.

Current Implementation

The Paideia Proposal began to be implemented at Skyline High School in Spring of 1981, when the principal brought together three teachers with a plan for scheduling their classes into two-hour blocks of time, long enough for conducting maieutic seminars. Since high schools approach efficiency in didactic instruction far more than coaching or maieutic, Skyline's "entering wedge" was the maieutic seminar.

The traditional English IV and American Government classes were transformed into the Block Program, with the infusion of the arts and humanities as the third component. Students met two hours per day, five days a week, and earned *three* credits for English and Government graduation requirements.

This plan provided four hours of lecture per week, two hours of coaching, and four hours of seminar per week—with variations. The Block Program is so structured that the students are exposed to different seminar leaders each week, emphasizing government, the arts, humanities, and literature. Students' learning is measured by oral questioning, and an oral dissertation on several ideas supported by literature. As well, students write papers which include each of the major ideas in the three columns (*Proposal*, p. 23).

105

Teacher training is conducted by seminar and coaching sessions. Teachers meet with the principal and conduct seminars on methodology and content described in *The Paideia Proposal*. Additionally, they have observed Mortimer Adler conduct seminars at Skyline.

These teachers bring with them twenty-five years of teaching experience, *personal* seminar experience, and advanced training in their fields (considerably more teacher training than most teachers possess).

The coaching has been done by the three teachers involved and by the principal in regular sessions. Students' writing is read and discussed with the principal as well as the teachers, for example. Students are thus exposed to four teachers.

The experience of analytical and critical thinking through active participation on the part of students—and the staff—has caused students to rate the program the most enlightening and successful educational experience they have had.

The reading list which forms the basis for the seminars includes: *Iliad, Oresteia Trilogy, Declaration of Independence, Plato's Republic, Nicomachean Ethics, The Divine Comedy, The Canterbury Tales, The Prince,* Montaigne's *Essays, Hamlet, Tartuffe, The Social Contract, The Misanthrope, Candide, Madame Bovary, Crime and Punishment, The Secret Sharer, Pride and Prejudice, Wuthering Heights, An Enemy of the People, 1984, St. Augustine's Confessions,* and *Walden.*

Plans for Future Implementation

The positive student feedback from the pilot, in effect for two years, motivates an expansion of staff and student participation. In the plan for total implementation (a five-year plan), Skyline intends to include feeder elementary and junior high schools. For next year, however, the principal has selected twenty-five members of his school's staff to learn how to use the maieutic approach and Socratic techniques.

The additional teachers who will be concerned with conducting seminars are now being involved as participants in seminars themselves—at the listening and responding end of Socratic questioning. These teachers are also being given some coaching in the techniques of coaching—something not done for them in the schools or departments of education in which they were trained.

The original student groups involved high school seniors. These are being expanded to include tenth and eleventh, as well as twelfth grade students. As well, the original teachers will broaden their program to involve whole classes of hitherto less academically successful students.

Expanded programs will include two-hour blocks structured according to the three columns at 10th, 11th and 12th grade levels in Science and Mathematics; English/History/Humanities; Foreign Language/Art; Manual Arts/Mathematics.

Students can become involved in all three blocks, and summer reading lists are being prepared for next year's participants. The structure of the expanded program will deviate from the traditional schedule as follows:

Monday, Tuesday		Didactic instruction, lectures and responses; textbooks, films, etc.
Thursday, Friday		(Continue to use the good practices already implemented.)
Wednesday	Period 1 *Writing*	1 hour 45 minutes coaching session (written work) supervised practice.
	Period 3 *Seminar Oral*	1 hour 45 minutes maieutic seminar (oral work) discussion of books—contents—ideas.
	Period 5 *Coaching Oral*	1 hour 45 minutes coaching—speaking *listening in content areas*. How to converse and listen in content area.

107

This program will involve approximately 400 students and some 20 teachers, who are themselves being trained as described above.

During the course of next year, Skyline plans to involve feeder elementary and junior high school staff and students as observers and periodic participants, in preparation for subsequent expansion.

To say that *The Paideia Proposal* has proved successful is an understatement. The students' enthusiasm and awakening to learning which result from the opportunity to participate actively in their own learning is overwhelming.

The "change in direction—the ascent in quality," as Adler describes it, is affecting participants fundamentally. One begins to see education happening in a public school.

Appendix III

Statement by Theodore R. Sizer, formerly Dean of the Harvard Graduate School of Education and Headmaster of Phillips Academy at Andover, and currently Chairman of a study of American high schools.

How should one begin planning for a Paideia school, or a Paideia program within a school? As no two schools will be alike, I can only make some general, procedural suggestions of steps that might be taken.

Suggested first step: Make sure that all involved in the project understand it and are committed to it, however skeptical one or another might be about some of its practical aspects. Those "involved" include the teachers and principals affected. Also involved are key central office administrators, school board members, representative influential parents of prospective students in the program, and, where older students are involved, these young people themselves.

This process will take time. Many think *Paideia* is a curriculum— a set of required courses that merely have to be plugged in. They have to be persuaded that Paideia is *not* a detailed One Best Curriculum, but rather a set of principles, a framework, and a process. Those using the principles have the responsibility of crafting the critical details of the program, in ways appropriate to their own communities.

All involved have to believe that all children can be educated, that they can use their minds well, that they can be motivated and inspired to do so, and that all are properly served by the overarching *Paideia* framework. They must understand the pedagogies involved and have some experience with them. I repeat: this process takes time and patience. To rush into it, or steamroll those involved, or to impose Paideia by *ukase* is to guarantee failure.

109

Suggested second step: Focus on outcomes: what knowledge, skills, and understandings must be demonstrated, at which levels, and how can students most effectively exhibit their mastery? Here again the framework of *The Paideia Proposal* is a starting point, no more than that. The specifics of a particular community's objectives need to be identified and sorted out.

A good way to do this is to establish tentative "checkpoints" over the sequence of years planned for the school, and to work out examinations for each. One might select, say, the third, sixth, ninth, and twelfth grade levels (knowing full well that students will reach these different levels at different paces, and thus at moderately differing ages).

This process tends to bring disagreement about ends and fuzzy thinking about means to the surface; the very specificity of examinations focuses issues and sharpens priorities. The framework of the three columns is crucial here, as it identifies the knowledge, the skills, and the understandings to be forwarded, and it gives general guidance for the organization of subject-matter. The specifics must be done locally, as no two schools are precisely the same, nor should they be.

The process of examination-writing (which is in large part an exercise in detailed goal-setting) again takes time. It cannot be rushed, and no outside authority can do it for the staff that must use it. The traditional system of sending down from On High detailed syllabi to teachers simply will not work. If the effort is to succeed, the participants in a Paideia School must have a critical stake in its design. Outside agencies can help (just as we hope our *Proposal* helps), but they must remain the supporting actors.

Suggested third step: Once the "checkpoint" goals (in the form of tentative, prototypical examinations) are developed, the task of evolving the means to achieve them follows.

The dangers here are numerous, as the weight of tradition and the narrow, specialist education of most middle and high school teachers will conspire to force the program, at least for older students, into familiar 50-minute long sessions dominated by teacher "telling."

A good tactical protection against this is to focus first on the development of intellectual skills and the improvement of understanding. The achievement of these requires a break from many traditional modes. "Coaching" and "questioning" will lay claim to now seldom-used teacher skills and to different forms of student grouping. Once one break is made, others will follow more easily.

The labels we use for certain subjects, and the expectations behind those labels accrued over the years, present similar hazards. For example, the word "English" as used in such phrases as "English course," "English teacher," or "English department" is treacherously ambiguous. It sometimes refers to coaching writing and reading skills, and less often to the correlative skills for speaking and listening. When "English teacher" refers to a teacher of skills, it should mean coaching in all basic skills of the language arts, not just writing.

An "English course" sometimes means a course of didactic instruction in the history of English literature, and sometimes it passes from that into a discussion of important literary works in the English language. It seldom becomes a Socratically conducted discussion of all forms of literature in all fields of subject-matter—not merely poetry or imaginative literature, but also significant books in history, in philosophy, in mathematics, in natural science, and so on.

Only when "literature" stands for books of every variety, some written in English or some in other languages, does the reference to literature in Column One relate didactic instruction there to Socratic teaching concerned with the reading and discussion of books in Column Three.

Only when "language" stands for both English and a foreign language and only when the language arts include all four of the basic operations—reading as well as writing, listening as well as speaking—does the reference to didactic instruction in language in Column One relate to coaching the language arts as prescribed in Column Two.

Thus, the conventionally styled "English" teacher will find himself or herself on often quite unfamiliar ground in a Paideia school. Allowances must be made for that reality.

So, too, didactic instruction in mathematics or science, as prescribed in Column One, must be related to coaching of the operational skills in these areas of subject-matter, as prescribed in Column Two. Many of the same problems found in language and literature emerge here. Again, accommodations will be necessary.

Again, this process will take time. When there is a rush to get something "started," and only a summer, let us say, with only a part of the staff engaged in planning, the result will invariably be a botched effort. When faced with incomplete plans and ambiguous new directions, all of us naturally retreat into what we are accustomed to do—to traditional patterns.

Only a comprehensive plan, fully understood by the staff, of its own making, and specified down to a detailed, practical level, is a worthwhile effort. Some will say that this is impossible, that "there isn't time and money for planning." I respond by asking if they would take the same attitude toward the procedures in an operating room as they are being wheeled in for spinal surgery. Good planning in both schools and operating theatres simply cannot be impossible.

Suggested fourth step: Once under way, time and the means to track the progress of the program must be built in. Teachers will be threatened, inspired, exhausted, energized, and overwhelmed with the new ways of working. They will need time and opportunity to talk through what their experience is, to re-think approaches which seem not to be working as intended, and to make adjustments in the program. To assume that time for planning and planning again ceases when school starts is a mistake that will harm the program.

112

Such are four steps for consideration. The task can be made easier by starting with one age group—say, four-to-six-year-olds, and by planning the program for them as the years go by. Starting with a "pilot" group within a more conventional setting can also be helpful, as long as the routines of the parent institution do not critically intrude.

My advice ultimately rests on five key points. (1) Believe that all children can and want to use their minds, and that our expectations for them must be optimistic ones. (2) Pay careful attention to the three modes of learning and the three modes of teaching, and remember that the ultimate objective is to "produce" young people who know how to learn for themselves. (3) Develop a sensible local program that fits the Paideia framework, and engage in planning all those who will work in it. (4) Be patient: good school plans take time. (5) Keep a sense of humor and do not abandon your idealism.